The Fundamentals of Illustration
Lawrence Zeegen/Crush

ava
academia

An AVA Book

Published by AVA Publishing SA
Rue des Fontenailles 16
Case Postale
1000 Lausanne 6
Switzerland
Tel: +41 786 005 109
Email: enquiries@avabooks.ch

Distributed by Thames & Hudson (ex-North America)
181a High Holborn
London WC1V 7QX
United Kingdom
Tel: +44 20 7845 5000
Fax: +44 20 7845 5055
Email: sales@thameshudson.co.uk
www.thamesandhudson.com

Distributed in the USA and Canada by:
Ingram Publisher Services Inc.
1 Ingram Blvd.
La Vergne TN 37086
USA
Tel: +1 866 400 5351
Fax: +1 800 838 1149
Email: customer.service@ingrampublisherservices.com

English Language Support Office
AVA Publishing (UK) Ltd.
Tel: +44 1903 204 455
Email: enquiries@avabooks.ch

ISBN 978-2-940373-33-8

10 9 8 7 6

Design by Crush Design and Art Direction
www.crushed.co.uk / info@crushed.co.uk

Production by AVA Book Production Pte. Ltd., Singapore
Tel: +65 6334 8173
Fax: +65 6259 9830
Email: production@avabooks.com.sg

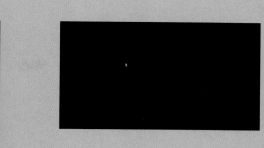

Lawrence Zeegen/Crush

The Fundamentals
of Illustration

Ethical:
aware-
ness/
reflect-
ion/
debate

academia

Contents

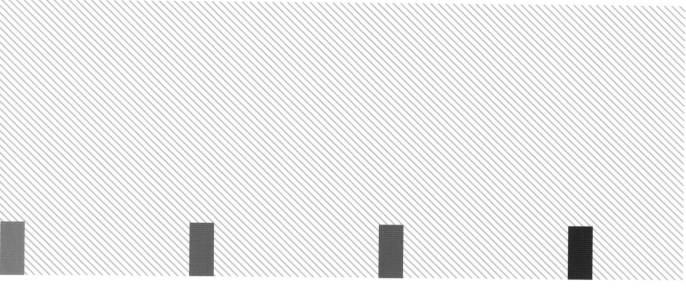

3
FROM OUTCOMES TO OUTLETS

4
MAKING IT HAPPEN

5
PRODUCTION

6
CONCLUSION

1. Each spread has **numbered images** – where numbers are backed by coloured boxes; they form part of a group of images that illustrates a point – look for caption colour bars of the same colour nearby.

2. **Pull-quotes** highlight key points of importance from the body text – locate these for examples of interest.

3. **Interviews** feature expertise, in-depth knowledge and advice from some of today's finest illustrators from across the globe.

1. Key information can be found in **box-outs** – find diagrammatical explanations, time-lines, easy-to-follow bullet points, as well as pros and cons within these graphic devices.

2. Related images are discussed using **group captions** – these pull together facts that work across the group of images.

3. **Images** used to illustrate the text represent examples of work from many of the best international illustrators working commercially today.

1. In-depth discussion of working methods and best practice including professional advice guidance is covered in the book's **body copy**.

2. Interesting facts and information that put the body copy in context is featured in **caption specific** and caption **copy**.

How to Get the Most from this Book

'The Fundamentals of Illustration' is intended as a comprehensive guide for illustrators, designers and those who commission illustration. Investigating the generation of ideas, interpretation of the brief, analogue and digital working methods, and the art of self-promotion through examples of contemporary practice, this book offers a unique resource and insight into illustration.

Professor George Hardie has worked as a 'jobbing' illustrator for 35 years. He formed NTA Studios in 1973 and worked closely with Hipgnosis designing for the music industry, creating sleeves for Pink Floyd, Led Zeppelin and Black Sabbath. Hardie has worked with clients internationally, 13 to date, and has created stamps for the Royal Mail. He is a member of the Alliance Graphique Internationale, Double Crown Club and Artworkers Guild.

Foreword

You enter a large, dark room and feel for the light. You find a bank of switches – row upon row. You switch one at random – a light illuminates a clean sheet of white paper lying untouched on a table. You try another – a biro doodle on the back of an envelope is exposed. Next, light falls on a scientific diagram.

A further switch, surprisingly, turns on a projector and an animation starts rolling. You switch on others and a children's book appears. It is followed by a single tiny postage stamp, a framed drawing hanging on the wall lit from above, a row of labelled wine bottles, a poster, a map, a comic, a model stage set and a wood engraving.

A computer screen lights up. An exquisite alphabet appears. A further switch reveals a group of 3D characters. The next, a drawing of a pair of shoes in a magazine.

The last switch shines a spotlight on to the switchboard. Each switch has a label. You read them: Communication. Opinion. Drawing. Narrative. Pattern. Idea. Fashion. Movement. Promotion. Media. Recompense. Style. Tax. Composition. Sequence. Abstraction. Education. Collection. Medium.

The door to this mysterious and exciting room, like the cover of this book, has the word 'Illustration' lettered upon it. Underneath, in brackets, you read 'To illuminate or cast light on a subject'.

Lawrence Zeegen has succeeded in doing just this in an intelligent, elegant and original way. Using examples that will stand the test of time, he casts light on the professionalism, philosophy and practicality of this vast subject.

Professor George Hardie

INTRODUCTION

1.

2.

5.

3.

6.

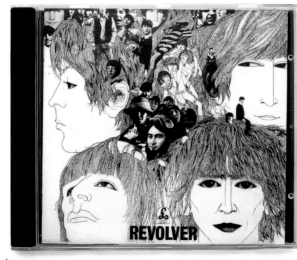

4.

Illustration is a dirty word, or at least was until recently. Neither truly accepted by the art establishment nor the design industry, illustration has battled on regardless. Derided as whimsical by artists and arty by designers, illustration had found itself existing in a no-man's-land between the two. In education the discipline has fared no better rarely given more than just studio space, the student illustrator has learnt to bend the rules and break across borders to gain access to facilities and equipment to facilitate their work. Life as an illustrator is not for the faint-hearted and it takes massive determination to face the demands and rigours of a career choice that can feel vastly unsupported. But, against these odds, the discipline has mounted an impressive return to form; how and why?

According to The National Museum of Illustration in Rhode Island, USA, 'Illustrators combine personal expression with pictorial representation in order to convey ideas' – a useful description certainly, but one that falls short of fully capturing the essence of what the subject is or has been about. Describing the 'golden era', when magazines such as the Saturday Evening Post scoured the studios for great illustrators, the design writer and art director Steven Heller stated that 'illustration was the people's art'. This sentiment was echoed by the National Museum of Illustration – 'illustration serves as a reservoir of our social and cultural history', even going on to state – 'Illustration is therefore, a significant and enduring art form'.

It is illustrated images that capture the imagination, that remain with the viewer and that inextricably tie moments in one's personal history with the present. From the moment that small children are introduced to illustrated books through to their admiring record and CD sleeves of their teens and early twenties, illustrations play a part in defining important moments and periods in time. On a grander scale, it is fair to say that illustration has recorded man's achievements, interpreting them in a way not possible before the birth of photography. 'Look at the paintings of Pompeii', stresses Milton Glaser – cofounder of Pushpin Studios in New York, in 'The Education of the Illustrator' – 'the aboriginal wall paintings of Australia, the great frescos of Italy, and you understand a moment of time, and the belief systems of the population'. Contemporary illustration may work in less majestic surroundings, but its roots within the magazine racks, bookshelves and record collections of our homes stand as testament to the importance we place on the art and craft of the discipline.

Finding the exact point in time that contemporary illustration was kick-started is not an easy task. The very term 'contemporary' implies modern, current, up-to-date, fashionable and present-day, so peering too far back into a dim and distant past may draw into the frame images that today's audience would struggle to recognise or remember. If a line is drawn in the sand marking the halfway point in the last century for example, classic illustrated posters for the Second World War campaign by Tom Eckersley, or his amazing posters for Guinness, have to be ignored, having been created in the 1940s. The same treatment must then be applied to much of the work of Abram Games, although his iconic posters for the London Underground would slip into the list, having been produced in the early 1950s. Norman Rockwell's work for the Saturday Evening Post in the US would have to be refused entry, as would Ben Shahn's World War II posters. Saul Steinberg's work for New Yorker magazine, having emigrated to New York in 1951 from Bucharest via Milan, would make the grade, as would Edward Bawden's London Underground posters and Ronald Searle's illustrations for Punch magazine in the UK. For many that grew up in the 1960s and 1970s, however, the first truly contemporary illustrators came from a new generation of image-makers.

The 1960s witnessed an unprecedented rise in consumerism as the post-war 'baby boomers' approached life with an optimism and enthusiasm not seen before. Teenagers came of age: youth movements sprang up and with them the need for a graphic visual language to identify with. Psychedelia, Op Art and Pop Art all put the visual arts firmly on the map. Here was the start of a fresh, forward-thinking new era and illustrated images helped in defining the look of the decade.

It was probably the Beatles that gave popular culture during the sixties some of its most memorable illustrative images; from the Klaus Voormann sleeve for 'Revolver' in 1965, to the animated classic of 'Yellow Submarine' created from Heinz Edelmann's original drawings and on to the must-have book – 'The Beatles Illustrated Lyrics' by Alan Aldridge published in 1969. It was, however, the use of artist and illustrator, Peter Blake in 1967, who combined a photographic and illustrative approach for the creation of the sleeve for 'Sgt. Pepper's Lonely Hearts Club Band' that ensured the Beatles' status of forward-thinking creative directors as well as musicians.

7.

1. Rick Griffin
'Aoxomoxoa' by The Grateful Dead
Warner Brothers, 1969

2. Ian Beck
'Goodbye Yellow Brick Road' by Elton John
Rocket, 1973

3. George Hardie and Hipgnosis
'The Dark Side of The Moon' by Pink Floyd
EMI, 1973

4. Peter Blake
'Sgt. Pepper's Lonely Hearts Club Band' by
The Beatles
Parlophone, 1967

5. Robert Crumb
'Cheap Thrills' by Big Brother & The
Holding Company
CBS, 1967

6. Klaus Voormann
'Revolver' by The Beatles
Parlophone, 1966

7. David Pelham
'A Clockwork Orange' by Anthony Burgess
Penguin Books, 1974

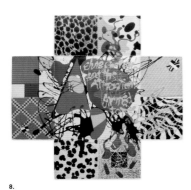

8.

9.

10.

Iconic illustrated images that mark the 1960s out as being a truly inspirational decade include Martin Sharp's covers for Oz, a satirical underground magazine with its roots in Sydney before being moved to London in 1966, and his poster for Bob Dylan the following year. Another Dylan poster, created the other side of the Atlantic by Milton Glaser in 1996, captures his hair as a pattern of psychedelic swirls. Robert Crumb's 'Fritz the Cat' cartoons, Michael English's poster for Jimi Hendrix, Victor Moscoso's covers for 'Zap Comix' and Rick Griffin's sleeves for The Grateful Dead all lent a graphic edge to the decade and are remembered by those that grew up then, reinforcing the gap between the pre-war and post-war generations.

As the 1960s faded away and the 1970s emerged as the decade that taste forgot, a new graphic sensibility began to take shape. Influenced by the drugs that had engulfed the hippy years of the late-1960s, work took on the visual aesthetics of fantasy and science fiction in the illustrations by Roger Dean and Peter Jones. With the Hipgnosis sleeve for Pink Floyd's 'Dark Side of The Moon', the surreal photo-montage of Tadanori Yokoo's sleeve for the Miles Davis album 'Agharta' and Ian Beck's cover for Elton John's 'Goodbye Yellow Brick Road', the early to mid-1970s was a minefield of graphic languages.

It was the hard-edged sound of the street, and punk later in the decade, that influenced some notable changes to the visual landscape. With a new urban, gritty, energetic sound came a raw, tougher approach to design with the 'cut-and-paste' graphic work for bands such as the Sex Pistols and The Clash. As punk and new wave adopted harder illustrative styles, designers like Barney Bubbles and his work for Elvis Costello, Ian Dury and The Damned and Russell Mills with projects for Penetration and Roger Eno, demonstrated a disregard for all that come before.

Throughout the 1980s and 1990s illustration's popularity rose and fell in equal measures. Memorable images by Ian Pollock for the National Theatre production of 'King Lear' vie alongside Pierre Le-Tan's masterly crafted covers for

The New Yorker, whilst Brad Holland's atmospheric painted illustrations for numerous magazines, compete with work by Glynn Boyd Harte, Chloe Cheese, Dan Fern, Seymour Chwast, Paul Hogarth, Peter Till, George Hardie, Bush Holyhead, Graham Rawle and Brian Grimwood. Perhaps best-known for their work spanning these decades are Gerald Scarfe for Pink Floyd's 'The Wall' and Ralph Steadman's images for 'Fear and Loathing in Las Vegas' by Hunter S. Thompson. The 1980s were a prolific time and despite cooling down in the 1990s as the last days of an analogue discipline gave way to a rebirth, rejuvenated by the possibilities of the digital, illustration continued to capture the moment.

So what of life as an illustrator in the 21st century? Why the huge interest in following a career that can take years to break into, only to fizzle out in an instant? Why endure the possible rejection of a negative portfolio review or the aggravation of chasing an accounts department hell-bent on ignoring requests for payment months after an invoice was first overdue? It has more to do with the desire to communicate, to create images and see that work in print. The rush of opening a magazine to see your own work, witnessing people reading a book on the tube or subway that you created the cover illustration for, or passing a billboard ad campaign with your drawings on is truly undeniable.

Getting ahead in illustration takes commitment, personality and talent. It is unlikely that an illustrator lacking in any one of these areas will pick up commissions and, toughest of all, still be working in five years' time. Developing a personal visual language, getting to grips with materials and understanding the ins and outs of the industry is only part of the story, to succeed, you'll need some insider info – and you're holding it in your hands.

11.

12.

8. Barney Bubbles and Bazooka
'Armed Forces' by Elvis Costello and the Attractions
F-Beat, 1979

9. Russell Mills and Robert Mason
'Moving Targets' by Penetration
Virgin, 1978

10. Stanley Donwood
'OK Computer' by Radiohead
Parlophone, 1997

11. Milton Glaser
Bob Dylan Poster (on T-shirt)
Pushpin, 1966

12. Graham Rawle
'Graham Rawle's Lost Consonants'
The Guardian, 2003

1. COMMUNICATING IDEAS

The essence of an illustration is in the thinking – the ideas and concepts that form the backbone of what an image is trying to communicate. Bringing life and a visual form to a text or message is the role of the illustrator – the best in the business combine smart analytical thinking with finely-tuned practical skills to create images that have something to say, and the ways and means to say it.

The Blank Sheet of Paper

There is nothing quite so disconcerting as the starkness of a blank sheet of paper or the glare from an empty screen, particularly in between receiving a commission for a professional illustration and making your first mark. That mildly disconcerting feeling can swiftly progress into an uncomfortable sense of unease, not unlike the feelings brought about by being made, as a child, to stand outside the headmaster's office. Unchecked, fears combined with stress can turn to sheer panic, with further symptoms of nausea, palpitations and hot and cold flushes becoming increasingly evident. In these circumstances, the only satisfactory cure is an idea.

Realising your idea by putting pencil to paper or mouse to screen is the first step of the journey towards executing an illustration. Understanding how ideas take shape, and how to assist the process when they don't flow as readily as one would like, is crucial if working in illustration is to be a fruitful experience rather than a chore.

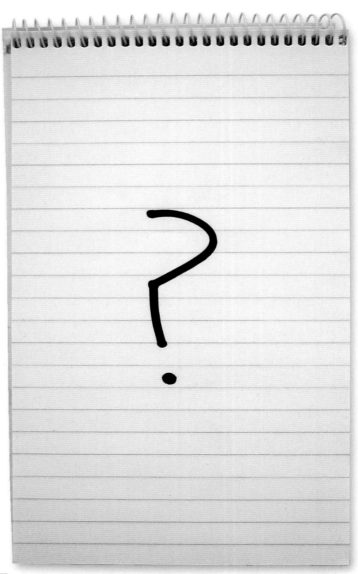

1.

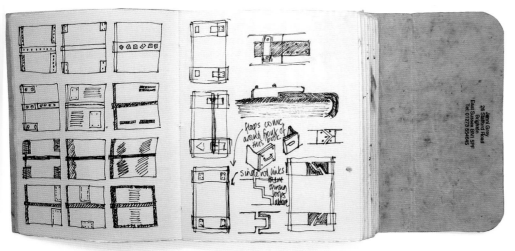

Ideas Generation

1. The starting point

Facing a blank sheet of paper at the start of a new project can be the most stressful aspect of a commission.

2. Sketchbook spreads
Jenni Grey, 2005

Generating ideas is part of the illustrator's role and the first place many turn to in order to start the process is the sketchbook. A unique relationship can develop between the artist/illustrator and their sketchbooks – here is a place where the communication is more personal, where the only audience is the artist themselves, and where pure experimentation with concepts and ideas can begin.

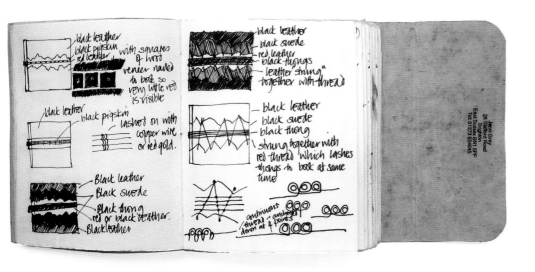

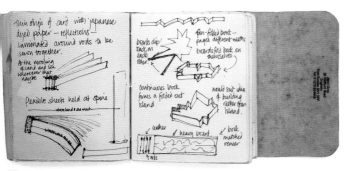

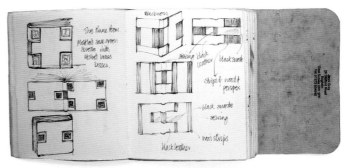

2.

Why Ideas?

A common misconception amongst student illustrators is that once a 'style' or method of working has been arrived at, there is little more to learn about the craft of illustration. Of course, technique and skills are absolutely invaluable, as is having an approach that could be considered unique. Yet just as important is the ability to create images that are underpinned with strong creative thinking and that have problem-solving ideas at the heart of the solution.

Illustration at its worst is merely a page-filler that might look good, but fails to give any knowledge of the subject that it illustrates. At its best, illustration encourages the viewer to think, to draw more from the text than first meets the eye and to comprehend a greater and more in-depth understanding of the subject. Great illustrations are like great stories and narratives – they require the viewer to become actively involved in order to fully comprehend the message. The concept may appear hidden at first, but communicates successfully when the viewer disseminates the image. Great illustration marries excellence in craft, skill and creative thinking.

Just as important is the ability to create images that are underpinned with strong creative thinking and that have problem-solving ideas at the heart of the solution.

1.

Just as trends in fashion or music ebb and flow, so too do styles in illustration. An illustrator recognised for a particular way of working may have a fantastically busy year professionally, only to find that as the commissions start to dry up they have fallen out of fashion. Keeping abreast of changes stylistically can help the illustrator stay one step ahead of the competition. However, creating images that resonate with creative ideas helps to produce a body of work that is timeless and doesn't rely on the whims of fashion in design and illustration.

Planning a career in illustration is anything but an exact science and there are no guarantees of longevity. However, many of the illustrators that have survived the test of time, working across a number of decades as opposed to just a number of years, have produced images that require more than just a passing glance from the viewer. Combining strong ideas with excellent execution can ensure an audience continues to appreciate the work of an illustrator, long after fashions and trends have moved on.

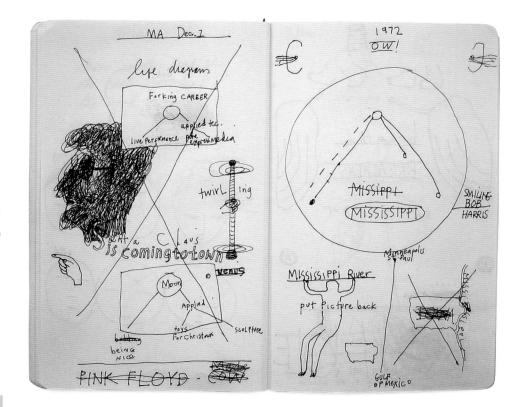

The Investigation of Ideas

• Use a sketchbook to record ideas and thoughts in an intuitive and automatic fashion – don't worry about how the ideas look at this stage.

• Carry a sketchbook and pen or pencil at all times – inspiration can occur in the unlikeliest places so it pays to be prepared.

• Jot down your thoughts using written as well as visual language, whichever best suits the thinking.

• Put down enough information to remind you of ideas, months or even years hence.

• Date and time your entries – this will help you to remember the context of what you were thinking at the time.

• Make a note of locations, reference materials and book titles as well as writing down important quotes that might help.

Ideas Generation (II)

1 & 2. Sketchbook spreads
Margaret Huber, 2005

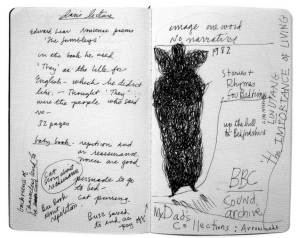

2.

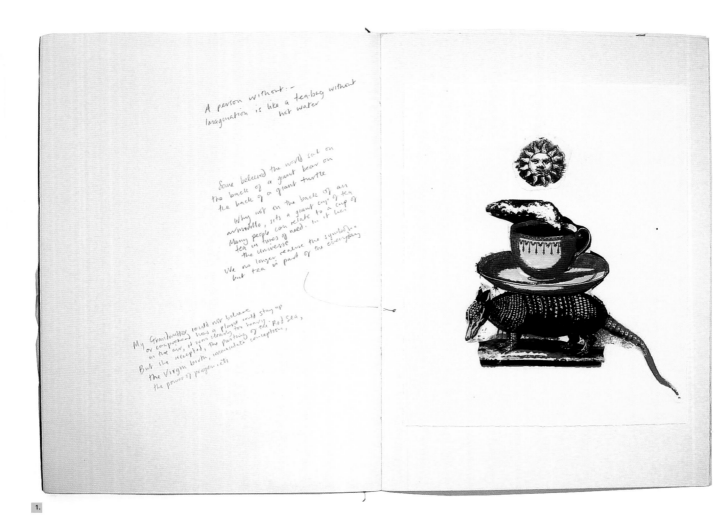

1.

At its best, illustration encourages the viewer to think, to draw more from the text than first meets the eye and to comprehend a greater and more in-depth understanding of the subject.

Ideas Generation (III)

**1 & 2. Sketchbook spreads
Gary Powell, 2005**

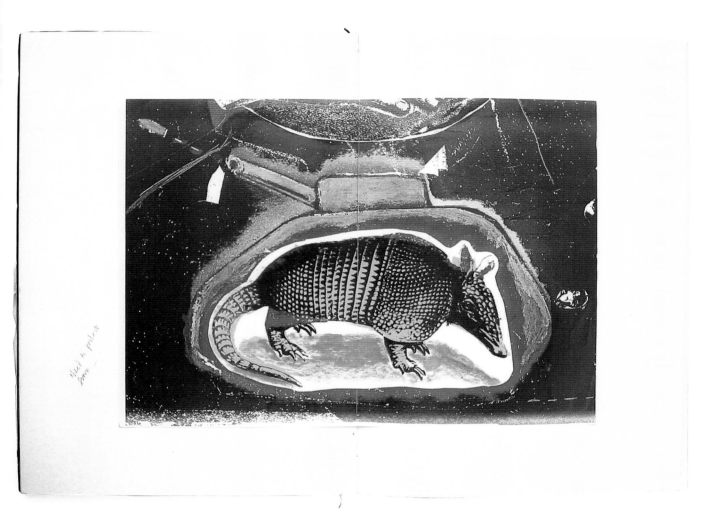

2.

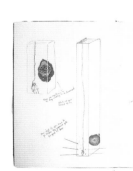

The Briefing

Mastering the ability to think creatively should not be shrouded in mystery. With some useful tips, most creative people can lay the foundations to ensure that they are best prepared to be creative in their thinking and start to generate interesting ideas. For the illustrator, the most important aspect of creative thinking starts with the briefing of a new project.

The initial briefing is the point at which basic information about the project must be gathered. Knowledge and understanding of the project is crucial. Being equipped with all of the relevant information required may appear obvious, but many fail to fully comprehend the importance of getting the facts correct at the start.

Knowing where the printed illustration is to appear, at what size, and whether it is to run in colour or black and white, should be basic aspects of the brief – if in doubt, ask. Being fully aware of the deadline for visuals and how much time is then available to complete the final artwork is crucial. If the work is for a new client – understanding the audience and researching previous copies of the publication can help build a picture of how your work may fit in and the range of illustration styles that the publication has used before.

Where possible, it is advisable to meet face-to-face with a client to receive a project brief, although this is often not realistic. Most briefings take place on the phone, via email or through agents. Unless the project is of a substantial size, a meeting of real people in real time is unlikely. For those rare face-to-face meetings it is vital to ensure that every aspect of a project is covered in detail. It is in these very early beginnings to a project that initial ideas can start to take shape.

1.

been broadly in line with forecast expectations and tender values. He explains, "We appoint a specialist life cycle modeller to forecast the life cycle replacement costs over the PFI concession periods. These costs reflect the proposed building materials being used and their manufacturers' recommended life guidelines."

But the majority of contracts are Design Build Finance & Operate (DBFO) and for these more value is contained in the FM services than in capital costs. So for instance a hospital with over 1,000 beds could require a £200 million capital spend and an FM contract of around £15 million a year for 25 or 30 years. And it is only now that we are a few years into the early PFI projects that anyone is able to make a judgement on whether FM services are giving clients value for money.

The first PFI hospital to open was the Darent Valley Hospital in Kent, and the National Audit Office (NAO) the independent body that certifies the accounts of government departments, has doubts about value for money here. First the positives. The facility opened two months early at the price agreed, and was awarded the maximum of three stars for performance. Refinancing resulted in a £33 million gain, 30% of which the contractors THC Dartford passed back to the Dartford and Gravesham NHS Trust, and shareholders are now enjoying an amazing return of 56%.

However, the Trust has agreed to extend the contract life by seven years to 35, and has accepted the possibility of increased liabilities in the event of early termination. And, what promises to cause a more immediate problem, some cleaning and catering services provided by Carillion were criticised. Comments like, "poor standards of cleanliness," and "little reference to work schedules," appear in the NAO's report. Mark Strathdene their spokesman says, "In our opinion the Trust could have given lower performance scores on the cleaning and catering. If they had, they would have gained greater deductions on the services."

Cleaning performance however is notoriously difficult to score, and comments like those quoted have to be put into perspective. However the water is now being muddied because the former FM at Darent Valley is bringing an unfair dismissal case before an employment tribunal under whistleblower guidelines. She alleges that she was victimised after questioning cleaning and catering performance. Symptomatic of any procurement contract's teething problems, or evidence of deeper ills? This remains to be seen. But Darent Valley will not be the only PFI project to come in for criticism.

Take prisons. Penalty points for poor performance deducted at Ashfield Prison and Young Offenders Unit resulted in financial deductions equal to three percent of the annual payment. There were resignations at senior management level and at one point the prison was taken out of the hands of Premier, the contractors, and run by the prison service before being handed back. Recruitment and staff retention were apparently a problem, resulting in insufficient staffing levels. And even when staffing was at full complement, the prison was only used at half capacity. In addition the NAO noted a high rate of assaults, a lack of policies and procedures, a lack of supervision and control, poor standards of physical accommodation and doubts about education.

However, before detractors claim that PFI has failed, the facilities and services procured in this way have to be compared with those built and run under traditional lines, and such comparison is difficult. Questioning the performance of contractors raises another point, and that is whether public sector bodies have the necessary expertise to manage

The possible meeting and associated conversation should act as a catalyst for the exploration of ideas. To ensure it is successful, be aware of the need to listen. Listening to the client talk about the project will help shape the direction of your visual solutions. Don't be afraid to ask questions, but then do make sure that you listen to the answers. No question that you ask will be inappropriate – you can never have too much information.

If you find that the client talks about the project in language that you don't comprehend, or in jargon that doesn't make sense – make sure that you ask them to rephrase what they are saying. Write down key points, but don't let your attention to writing stop you from listening. Clarify points later if you need to, but at this stage just get the broad brushstroke of the project.

When you leave the meeting or put down the phone, start by putting as much of the information learned on to paper as soon as possible. Write down every detail, every thought, idea and concept – however random, basic or crazy they may seem at the time. These notes will prove invaluable later as they will have been created from the fresh thoughts and instinctive responses you had to the project in the first instance.

Being armed with the facts can make a big difference – it makes sense to start generating ideas fortified with as much information as possible.

Understanding the Context

• Find out all details of the practical context; the size, position, the accompanying text and images and whether it will be in colour.

• Never start an illustration without knowing who will be looking at the outcome. Understanding the readership is key.

• Read previous issues of the publication you are illustrating for and note your response as you do so.

• If the image has been commissioned for a book jacket, having an insight into the author's previous books and how they have been illustrated can be useful.

• If working for the music industry, review the label's other issues, listen to the music being represented by your commission, and research the musician's likes and dislikes.

The possible meeting and associated conversation should act as a catalyst for the exploration of ideas. To ensure it is successful, be aware of the need to listen.

Comprehending the Brief

1. Example copy for editorial brief concerning a Private Finance Initiative

Start the process of any commissioned project by reading the brief. This example is copy (text) for an editorial illustration to accompany an article about government funding proposals that brings together a partnership between business and state – the private finance initiative. Although not an easy subject to instantly visualise, the key elements of the brief have been highlighted using a bright marker pen. Notes about the size that the image is to run in print as well as contact details and fee have been hastily scribbled on to the print-out.

Investigation of the Subject Matter

The illustrator frequently begins a project having been emailed text or copy from their client. This is particularly true for newspaper, magazine or book publishing commissions. A newspaper may have a regular IT feature or health page that requires illustrating, or a magazine may commission illustrators to produce images to accompany the texts of their regular columnists.

Whatever the type of commission, it is wise to investigate the subject matter of the text in as much depth as possible. Researching on the Internet, and in bookshops and libraries, should harvest more information than the text for the magazine or newspaper article can possibly cover. Having more information about the subject can throw new light on to possible avenues of thought.

It is useful to build a bigger picture but don't forget the original text. Get as much information as you can – obviously, the most important thing at the start of a project is to understand the subject that you are illustrating. Be careful though, remember that you are being commissioned to create an illustration that complements the text being published.

When an illustrator is busy with numerous commissions the greatest temptation is to place any new incoming projects to the bottom of the pile and ignore them until the impending deadline looms so close that it remains impossible to contemplate putting off the project any longer. For many freelance illustrators there is an in-built aversion to completing a job before the specified deadline, this is not due to laziness, but the fear of being without work. Being freelance means that there are times when one is busy and other times when one is without work, or 'in between projects', as actors like to describe unemployment. Having a backlog of work maintains the sense of full employment. This process of leaving projects until the very last minute is not conducive to creative thinking though.

It is wise to get to grips with a project as soon as possible. Often the best ideas will come when least expected – in the shower, on the bus, whilst cooking – but this can only happen if the project has been investigated, or at least the text has been digested, early on. Reading the text through thoroughly a few times in a quiet space, with a cup of coffee and a notepad and pen handy is the ideal way to start the creative process. Printing a second copy of the text and having it to hand in your bag with the notepad and pen, so that it can be called upon and referred to whenever there is a free moment makes real sense. Remember that a good idea can take shape anywhere.

Starting the process early on and filling the brain with as much related information about the subject matter as possible will kick-start the process of ideas generation. Try to be relaxed and have the confidence to recognise that good creative ideas can take time to form. Training the mind not to panic in the face of slow developments is a key aspect of the creative process. In essence, don't arrive at the blank sheet of paper or screen in an unprepared state – read the brief, understand your audience and arrive armed with your notes.

Making Notes

Everyone has a different approach to taking and making notes. Some like to scribble single words and phrases, others prefer to write their thoughts out in long hand, while others create a combination of sketches, and handwritten thoughts and explanations. Find the method that best suits your own purposes – use a sketchbook, or a notebook, sheets of A4 copier paper, write on to the printed brief itself, whichever method feels right.

Start by reading the brief or the text all the way through, as well as the notes that you made at the briefing meeting if it occurred, without trying to make notes. Of course, if ideas or thoughts spring to mind during this first read-through, get them briefly down on paper, but use the first read-through as simply an opportunity to gain an understanding of the story or article. It is very unlikely that you'll know nothing about the content of the text; the art director commissioning the illustration

Understanding the Context

1. Keywords from the copy referenced using a thesaurus and then Google's Image search

The key to the development of a strong visual solution is in understanding the context in which the illustration will appear. Gathering information about the context that your work will appear in is the most productive starting point – never start an illustration without knowing who will be looking at the outcome.

Often the text supplied as a brief will be the final edit, ignore typos and awkward sentences unless they prevent you from understanding the general content sufficiently to illustrate it.

➡

Education

apprenticeship, background, book learning, brainwashing, breeding, catechism, civilization, coaching, cultivation, culture, direction, discipline, drilling, edification, enlightenment, erudition, finish, guidance, improvement, inculcation, indoctrination, information, knowledge, learnedness, learning, literacy, nurture, pedagogy, preparation, propagandism, proselytism, reading, rearing, refinement, scholarship, schooling, science, study, teaching, training, tuition, tutelage, tutoring

Prisons

bastille, big cage, big house, big joint, big school, campus, can, clink, confinement, cooler, crossbar hotel, dungeon, greystone college, guardhouse, jail, joint, keep, lockup, pen, penal institution, penitentiary, reformatory, sent up, slam, slammer, statesville, stockade

Hospitals

academy, association, asylum, business, clinic, college, company, conservatory, establishment, fixture, foundation, guild, hospital, institute, institution, orphanage, school, seminar, seminary, society, system, university

Transport

carriage, carrier, carrying, carting, conveyance, conveying, conveyor, freightage, hauling, lift, movement, mover, moving, passage, removal, shipment, shipping, transfer, transference, transferring, transit, transportation, transporting, truckage, vehicle

Research Methodologies

• The Internet as a Research Tool

Just a fingertip away, the Internet has surpassed a trip to the second-hand bookshop or library for many illustrators. Websites are available that can throw up visual reference within an instant and can provide factual information in just a few clicks of the mouse. Download times have quickened as broadband has become the norm and on-screen visual research has never been so accessible or so in demand. Make sure you bookmark your favourite websites.

• Thesaurus

Words and word play can provide starting points as well as solutions for the illustrator looking to create visuals with grounding in language. An old-fashioned thesaurus housed on a bookshelf will work just as well as an on-line version. Interesting and challenging results can be found by simply spending some time investigating words and their meanings.

• Google

The most important research tool on the Web for both guidance to sites and spots where a subject is mentioned, Google's image-search facility is perfect for finding and discovering a range of both photographic and drawn images related to the keyword you are searching for.

• Spider Diagrams

Spider diagrams can be particularly useful when working with a complex set of problems or with information less easy to visually define. Start by making notes about the range of subjects or headings that you wish to investigate and then add notes and research about each as you work through them. Where you see links between subjects or potential ideas, create visual links that will help you later define and clarify your thoughts into more conclusive concepts.

1.

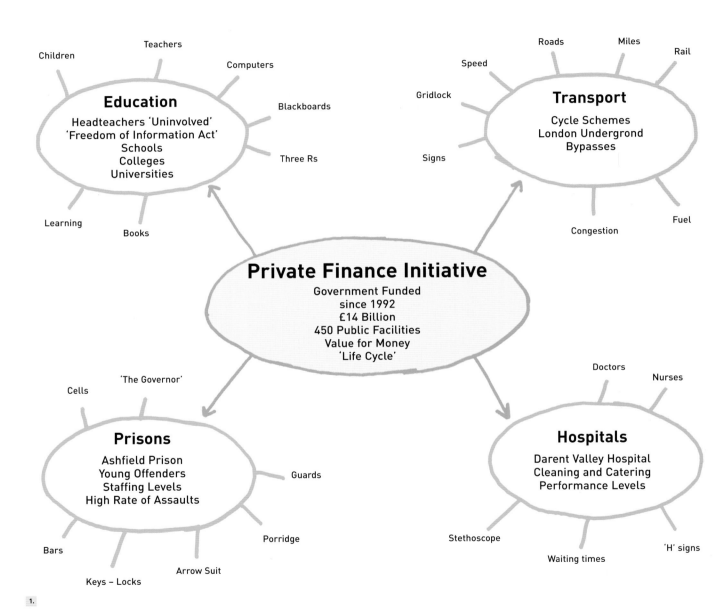

Education
Headteachers 'Uninvolved'
'Freedom of Information Act'
Schools
Colleges
Universities

Children
Teachers
Computers
Blackboards
Three Rs
Learning
Books

Transport
Cycle Schemes
London Undergrond
Bypasses

Speed
Gridlock
Roads
Miles
Rail
Signs
Congestion
Fuel

Private Finance Initiative
Government Funded
since 1992
£14 Billion
450 Public Facilities
Value for Money
'Life Cycle'

Prisons
Ashfield Prison
Young Offenders
Staffing Levels
High Rate of Assaults

'The Governor'
Cells
Guards
Bars
Keys – Locks
Arrow Suit
Porridge

Hospitals
Darent Valley Hospital
Cleaning and Catering
Performance Levels

Doctors
Nurses
Stethoscope
Waiting times
'H' signs

1.

Mood-boards

• Some illustrators like to start a project by creating a mood-board from sketches and collected ephemera. This approach is determined by the kind of project that has been commissioned. If a set of images is being produced, mood-boards can reflect the overall visual style of the work.

• Mood-boards may represent colours, shapes, tones and textures, but can also be used to group visual objects and to set the scene of the artwork. They can be useful reference points for the illustrator and act as excellent visual guides for clients too.

• Start a mood-board by collecting and visualising potential aspects and tape or tack them on to sheets of paper or board – foam board is useful for this, being lightweight yet rigid. Having your mood-board in front of you whilst working can assist the process too, allowing a constant reference point.

Connections

• Allow yourself to explore connections – it may be that seemingly unconnected words or visuals once brought together bring a new meaning or start a chain of other connections. Just the juxtaposition of two or three elements can lead an idea in a new direction – don't be afraid to experiment.

Understanding the Context (II)

1. Spider diagram

This example investigates the subject of the Private Finance Initiative – divided into the four main sections, this shows the relevant information under each heading.

Research and Ideas Sheets

• Collect words – use a written list to itemise everything that you can think of that is connected to the project. Use a highlighter pen to mark those words that seem potent and that may add something to your thinking.

• Cut up your lists and place the chosen words on to a fresh sheet of paper – tape them down and start to draw lines between words where you see possible links. Look for themes – both in thinking and in visual terms. New words and visuals will start to form, create them, write them down and add these to your diagram. Go down unexplored routes and see what happens – be spontaneous.

Metaphors

• Many successful illustrators use metaphors successfully in their work. A metaphor can be a word or an image that isn't to be read or viewed literally but makes a comparison. Using symbolism or figures of speech that do not represent real things can be described as a metaphor. Money doesn't really grow on trees, but as a metaphor we understand the point of the phrase. It is vital to understand your audience in this context; not all metaphors travel well. A commonly used European metaphor may not translate to an Asian audience and vice-versa, for example. If in doubt, check it out.

will have mentioned something of the content on the phone or in an email when asking if you would like to take on the commission.

Make sure that your interpretation of the text is clear – it may differ from the original thoughts you had about the project before you had a chance to read the text. This is quite normal, so it is always best to delay making any decisions, however small, about your illustration until you have read the text thoroughly.

During a second or third reading start to make notes. Don't worry about the shape that they take – these notes are not for an external audience, but will be useful reminders and pointers when you look back at them. Make sure that you understand and can comprehend your own notes – you may not return to them for a few days and they need to be easily referenced and used. Use a highlighter pen to underline key areas of text – there will often be useful sections that summarise the overall points that the writer is making. Some illustrators find it useful to staple blank sheets of paper in between the sheets of text to jot notes and ideas on to.

The note-taking stage is purely to establish initial thoughts and the beginnings of connections and ideas. Don't panic if, during the first session, you find that nothing concrete has emerged. You will have fed through much information contained within the text and your mind will use this over the course of the next hours or, ideally, days.

First Visual Representation

The notes you have created are probably just single words or phrases, and perhaps a few key sentences. You may have also produced some very simple visuals. These visuals are unlikely to be anything more than scribbles, a visual form of note-taking, characterised by the simplicity of the line – a figure represented by a stick man, a building by a child-like drawing of a house etc. Recognise these drawings as the first stages towards visualising written language – they may not hold the key to producing the final illustration, but they are the stepping stones or building blocks towards later illustrations. Get into the habit of working this way – some find it easier than taking written notes – but just as in writing, ensure that you get enough detail down to remember exactly what the point of the drawings was.

In essence, don't arrive at the blank sheet of paper or screen in an unprepared state – read the brief, understand your audience and arrive armed with your notes.

Gathering Inspiration

Inspiration for projects and for the ideas that drive projects will not come from just researching the subject in hand. An illustrator must constantly be on the look out for inspiration and reference materials and resources. Most illustrators create their own archives of images and objects, organising their collections into folders, drawers and boxes. These collections can be incredible sources of inspiration.

The action of constantly looking and recording is very much part of the illustrator's lifestyle. Inspiration is everywhere, a cliché perhaps, but so very true. Finding time to dive into a second-hand bookshop or car boot sale, photographing a moment or mood, capturing a sentence uttered by a stranger overheard in a supermarket – these can all be inspirational and deserve their own space in an illustrator's archives.

It may be a simple combination of colours used in a piece of packaging, the way a figure is captured in a photograph or the texture of a used tram ticket from a childhood vacation that inspires – there is a sixth sense that illustrators develop when collecting and collating reference materials.

Setting up an archive of reference is an enjoyable process and although it can be time-consuming, it is a thoroughly worthwhile and useful aspect of the creative process. Being aware of your influences, and of the visual aesthetics that you respond well to, will lead successfully to gaining inspiration and ideas from the everyday.

The Sketchbook

A sketchbook is the illustrator's best friend. A sketchbook is not just for sketching and drawing in though, it should be a constant companion and the one item that the illustrator turns to to record and document notes, found images and all manner of inspirational material. Get into the habit of carrying it with you at all times, buy one that fits in your pocket or in a bag that you always use. Don't make the mistake of replacing your sketchbook

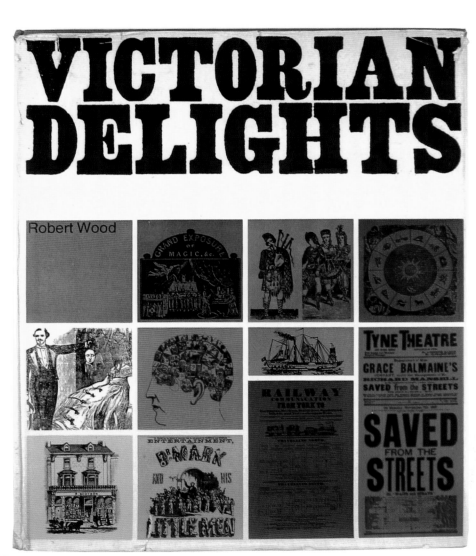

1.

2.

with a diary or a time-planner – they are different things. You should not have to schedule time to be creative, it should just occur, and when it does you need to be prepared.

Use your sketchbook to contain all that you record, don't worry about keeping it specifically for either personal or professional work – put everything in and you'll find that the two areas mix and merge. Draw, doodle, write and note-take whenever and wherever. Clip out findings from newspapers and magazines and tape them in, staple in ticket stubs and any kind of ephemera that you've found or collected. Stick in photographs, rescued pieces of photocopied images, stencils, stickers, flyers, cards... the list is endless.

The Project File

A file created for each project is another method of storing all related materials, ideas and inspirations as well as the formal paperwork relating to a project such as the brief, the contract and reference material supplied by the client. It is useful to create both a digital and analogue project file. Creating a new folder, saved on to your hard disk for all correspondence, copies of emails, and digital reference material is as important as a real-world version. Like an expanded and more focused version of the sketchbook, the project file can encompass everything that relates to, or that could relate to, the project in hand. ➤

Project Development Case Study (I)

1, 2. 'Victorian Delights'

3. 'Naive Painting'

These are some of the books used as reference by illustrator Jason Ford whilst working on a project to illustrate 'My East End', a short story by Gilda O'Neil set in Victorian London.

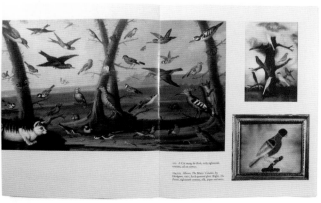

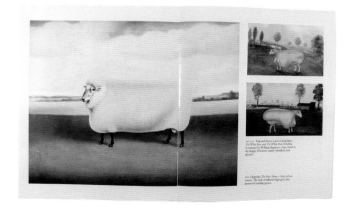

3.

A useful project file is one that houses every aspect of the project – from relevant pages torn from sketchbooks to a series of photographic reference images, and photocopies from second-hand books to print-outs from Google searches. It is this material that will assist in inspiring ideas – spread out all of your reference materials, notes and written and visual research in front of you whilst you work. The blank sheet of paper or screen will feel less daunting when surrounded by the visual material that has fed into your thinking.

The Creative Environment

Working in a positive environment can do wonders for the generation of creative ideas. Finding a calm, quiet space to retreat to works for most people. Turning the land-line off, silencing a mobile and quitting an email application will all help to ensure that your time is not interrupted by a constant flow of communication from the outside world. Turn off the radio, the CD player and the TV, and get prepared to think creatively.

Organising a work space, clearing the digital desktop and cleaning the real world desktop all help in metaphorically freeing up some fresh space in which to think. Empty the studio bin, open a window and let in some fresh air – make your environment fresh and it will help you reap the rewards.

Some people not only clean and clear, they also re-jig their work spaces at the start of a new project. They reposition their screen, tidy the spaghetti chaos of their computer cables and reorganise their bookcases. Archiving previous projects on to CD or DVD, or filing papers away into their relevant folders can be a real plus too, mentally helping to bring a conclusion to finished work before the fresh start of a brand new project.

Whilst many like to make a hot drink to relax with as they start the thinking process, plenty of others find creative realisation can come from actually leaving the studio environment and having a drink in a local coffee shop or café. There is something unique about sitting with a new project on the table with a pen in one hand and a frothy cappuccino in the other. Being away from normal distractions and focusing the mind on the job in hand can be hugely beneficial.

The more time that you spend working as an illustrator the more you can begin to recognise and then concentrate on the particular ways that best suit your approach to creative thinking. Learn to capitalise on the scenarios and locations that work most effectively for you. If your best ideas come during the afternoon, learn from this and use your mornings to work at other aspects of illustration – the filing, emailing, invoicing, marketing, etc.

Know the point when it is best that you walk away from the process of creating ideas – learn to accept when your creative juices are not flowing. Hitting a brick wall or a black hole – call a creative block what you like – is not fun, but it does happen to all of us and on a regular basis too. Banging your head against that wall will not help – getting out for a walk in the fresh air, wandering around an exhibition or catching a movie may be all you need to clear the mind and prepare yourself for another attempt. Knowing when to stop is as vital as knowing how to start.

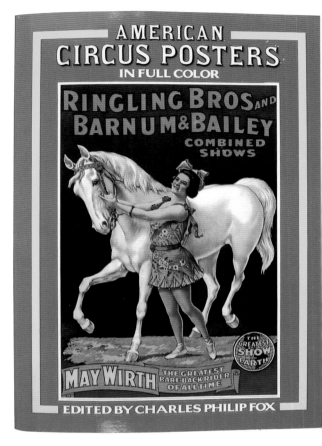

Most illustrators create their own archives of images and objects, organising their collections into folders, drawers and boxes. These collections can be incredible sources of inspiration.

1.

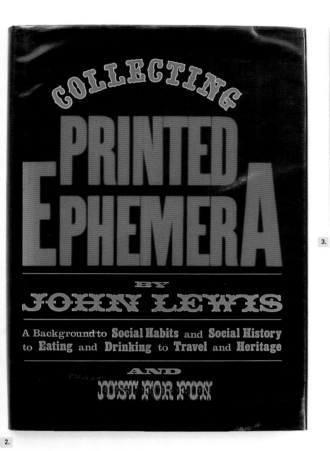

2.

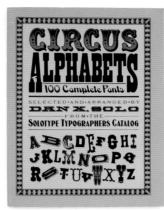

3.

Historical Research

Historical accuracy may not be a factor in most illustrations, but whenever a project calls for detailed visual information about a subject, it is wise to undertake some in-depth research. A little like a props and costume assistant in the theatre, the illustrator must ensure that every aspect of the image has undergone careful consideration and is correct for the time and the place.

The images on this page show how the illustrator referenced Victorian typography and poster art. Using expert information will ensure that mistakes are not made.

Project Development Case Study (I)

1. American circus posters

3. Circus alphabets

2 & 4. 'Collecting Printed Ephemera'

Additional material collected by Jason Ford to illustrate the short story 'My East End'.

4.

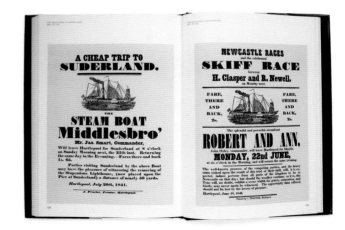

Brainstorming

You should now have a fully-formed project brief, your notes and interpretations from the briefing meeting, a sketchbook with early inspirations and thoughts, your research into the subject area as well as a project file and a fully functioning creative environment to work in. What you need now are some ideas!

Brainstorming can mean different things to different people. Simply expressed, it is the action of bringing together all of the research, notes, scribbles and thoughts and creating a series of bigger and more clearly defined ideas and paths to follow. Illustrators, unlike designers, will often have to brainstorm alone – illustration can be a lonely pursuit, as a solo activity there is only one person responsible for the final outcome. Of course, working with an art director or designer on a project can help, and discussing ideas should be very much part of the process, but ultimately there is only one person creating the initial ideas – you, the illustrator.

An onslaught of ideas and thoughts is the best way to describe how brainstorming should work. Get every idea and thought out and on to paper or screen. Keep your ideas flowing – good ideas, bad ideas, exciting, dull; let them all out. Just like a storm of heavy rain and gusting wind, your brain should be working overtime to produce as much as it can. Examine possibilities, explore links, twist meanings and subvert thoughts – anything goes. To make brainstorming work, you need to have the germs of ideas and lots of them.

The Investigation of Ideas

There are numerous ways that ideas can take shape after the initial brainstorming exercise. Recognising how to use the raw materials of creative thinking is the next stage in the process. Evaluating and editing your ideas can be just as difficult as the conception. Recognising a strong idea and working it through to a conclusion or following a thread of creative thinking to the next logical stage are all aspects of the process that improve with practice.

Embracing both a sense of realism – the image must communicate a message after all – and maintaining a high level of creativity can help translate the results of brainstorming into fully-formed concepts. Being realistic means that the wildest, most bizarre and unreadable ideas are kept away from production. Reminding yourself that the work must communicate is about being realistic. On the other hand, being creative means that the work stays fresh, takes risks and feels edgy – you are an artist after all. The right measure of realism and creativity is the goal.

Investigating your ideas and moving them into more concrete forms relies on a variety of means. Looking for connections, bringing words and images together or juxtaposing a number of elements can lead ideas into new directions. Viewing your concepts from an opposing angle can help too – a new perspective on the problem can be a fresh start. The use of colour can affect the mood of the image, whilst using metaphors can shift the emphasis of an idea or concept.

Risk-Taking in Illustration

The term 'risk' implies danger. Let's face it though – to the outside world the very idea that illustrators face risks and dangers on a daily basis is a little preposterous. Where risk-taking does come into effect in illustration is at the point where safe ideas and routes into a project are jettisoned in favour of opting for a less tried and tested route.

Opening new doors into the unknown and facing creative problems head-on without the safety net of familiarity is about being brave. Flying in the face of conformity and tackling problems within projects with new thinking and, at times, new ways of making images, can be the essence of what moves an illustrator's work forward – staving off the staleness of repetition.

Taking risks is a necessary aspect of creative thinking as well as in image-making itself. The future of an illustrator's career and the future of the discipline, rest on constantly moving forward and exploring new avenues of thinking.

1.

Exploring How Images Work

• Images help an audience perceive an idea and the role of illustration is to bring visual meaning to a given text. Images can be simple, complex, emotional, diagrammatic or documentary. Most importantly they should aim to present a point of view and they should make the viewer think. Images in the context of illustration should be unique – causing the viewer to see something in a way that they normally would not. They should also be emotional, bringing a sense of humanity to the viewer, as well as being appropriate and understandable.

• Visual communication relies on a mix of signs and symbols – how we 'read' images and how we decode their meanings occurs in a subconscious manner. The 'voice' inherent within an image is translated by an audience that have learnt how to understand and comprehend visual images through associations built up over the years.

• For an illustrator to bring these elements together into one image is no small achievement – all inextricably linked to a creative idea too, of course.

Project Development Case Study (III)

1. Initial sketches/visuals
'My East End' for Beat 2
Jason Ford, 2005

Early rough sketches identify a stylistic approach and aspects of the subject matter. These drawings are quick studies and a method for generating ideas through visual exploration. Nothing is decided nor rejected at this stage – everything still counts.

A stale illustrator will produce stale images. Often the greatest enemy of fresh original thinking is not the client, but the illustrator themselves. Having fallen into a formulaic 'style' of work, their approach to ideas, generation and thinking relies too heavily on clichés without pushing into cleverer and more challenging areas. It is wise to recognise the symptoms and work hard to ensure – through constant exposure to new materials, reference and research – that making illustrations remains a challenge.

Only through stepping into unchartered territories can new discoveries be made that will ultimately take one's work forward. On occasion, taking risks can lead to frustrations as not every attempt will come to fruition. Learning to recognise the pitfalls as well as the rewards is the first stage in facing the challenge however.

Ideas into Visuals and Roughs

It is one thing to get through the stages of ideas-generation intact and find a level of thinking and visual representation that you feel happy is solving the project brief. It is another stage of work to ensure that your client, and often their client, is as keen on your approach and has as much faith in the work as you do yourself.

It is extremely rare to be given complete freedom with a project, or be allowed to rush straight into creating finished artwork without supplying or presenting visuals that describe your thinking and the route that you'll be taking to construct that final artwork.

A visual or 'rough', as it is sometimes called, should ideally be a sketch that demonstrates loosely the elements that will appear in the work, although nothing will be completed in any great detail at this stage. Unfortunately, the ideal is now becoming threatened as more and more commissioners have started to expect visuals with more and more detail explored. This may be a reaction to the number of illustrators now creating images on screen. Clients can and will demand changes because they believe that the work can be modified by the illustrator easily on a computer. Expectations of more polished and finished visuals have been led by the growth in digital hardware and software – the equipment has created a culture where perfection is now a given.

1.

Project Development Case Study (IV)

1. Initial compositions
'My East End' for Beat 2
Jason Ford, 2005

The next stage in developing the illustration is to work with the independently created elements and visuals from the sketch stage, to build up a range of test compositions. It helps to give your compositions a space to occupy – a simple drawn rectangular line around the image shows the edge of the page or the image. Cropping into particular details can provide a more dynamic focus – practice this with two L-shaped pieces of card to frame different aspects of your work.

Explaining the Visual

More often than not, once a set of ideas has been fine-tuned into a definitive route forward, the visual will be emailed to the client for consideration. Obviously with bigger projects, a face-to-face meeting may well be set up, but 95% of all visuals will arrive without the benefit of a verbal explanation as accompaniment. Blankly sending a visual via email without a text explaining the route that you have taken with the brief can easily result in a negative response to your work. This will not always happen, but why take that risk? Courtesy, if nothing else, determines that it is a good idea to explain what your client is looking at.

Write a simple and concise explanation of the work explaining your thinking and detail what will change in the process of moving from visual to final artwork. Make reference to colours and textures that may change and note where elements will require further work – perhaps more detailed drawing will be required in some areas for example. Keep the commissioner in the loop by explaining your thinking and ideas a little. Highlight the key elements in the brief that you felt required exploring and expanding upon. Remember your client: the designer, art director or art buyer is likely to have to present your visual to someone else too. It may go

to an editor or a more senior creative director and it may have to be shown to a client that is not as visually aware as the designer that you are working with. If you are working on an advertising campaign, for example, your work may be presented to a team from the company that the advertising agency is working for. They could be the marketing department from a shoe or a washing detergent manufacturers – not necessarily the ideal audience to comprehend a rough visual working of an idea!

If you do get the opportunity to present your work in person, even at the visuals stage – leap at it. Getting some valuable experience of explaining your work is crucial. Offer to meet with clients if and when you can. Sitting down and talking face-to-face at both a briefing meeting and at the visuals stage can really iron out any slight misinterpretations from either side of the fence.

When speaking about your ideas and visual approach, be confident, speak clearly and use the visual to illustrate your explanations. If you get nervous in meeting situations, make some notes before you arrive – work out what you wish to say and don't be afraid to follow your notes. Be prepared to discuss and talk through

your work and to take on board relevant considerations and comments from those looking at your work. Try to react positively to advice and criticism about the work so far. Don't take any criticism of your thinking personally, further work may well be needed to help the illustration solve the brief in a way that the client is happy with. Take notes and be civil, but if you believe that you have valid points – make sure that you voice them: you will be respected for doing so. An illustrator should bring a different viewpoint and perspective to a project – stand up for yourself and have a strong belief in your contribution.

1.

2.

Project Development Case Study (IV)

**1 & 2. Test compositions
'My East End' for Beat 2
Jason Ford, 2005**

Here a more fully worked version of a composition starts to take shape. The image is still very much in the developmental stage – all the line work has been created with pencil on layout paper. This relies on rubbing out to remove unwanted elements or those that require redrawing.

Don't take any criticism of your thinking personally, further work may well be needed to help the illustration solve the brief in a way that the client is happy with.

1.

Project Development Case Study (V)

**1. Adding colour to the composition 'My East End' for Beat 2
Jason Ford, 2005**

A version created using detailed black line-work in place is scanned into Photoshop and colour digitally added. Two versions are tested – altering colours and saving new files being a simple process digitally. Note how the simple use of light and shade on the clouds, for example, gives the image a greater depth and sense of perspective.

Project Development Case Study (VI)

1. Client approval
'My East End' for Beat 2
Jason Ford, 2005

Even at what appears to be such a late
stage in the development of the work,
the client requested changes, wanting
the image to have a more modern,
upbeat and comical feel. Further black-
and-white developmental sketches were
produced and shown to the client before
commencing the final artwork. The final
piece certainly has a more engaging feel,
but still reflects the research and
investigation conducted earlier.

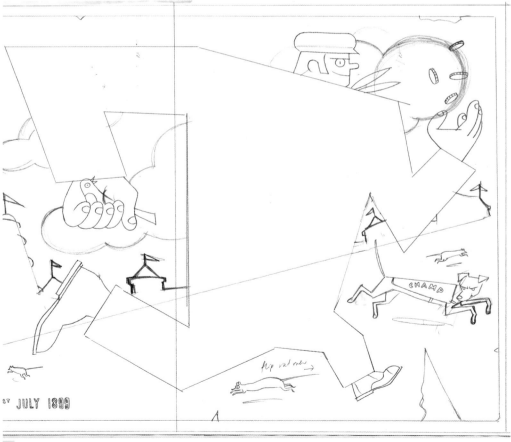

1.

Longevity

Ensuring that you develop a long-standing career in illustration can't be reduced down to just one or two factors. Like many things, it can be a mixture of talent, luck and circumstances – right place, right time. Increasing the chances of a successful and lengthy career can, however, be accomplished.

Working hard at creating images that have a personality, have something to say and can communicate to a given audience, can be a big part of the game plan. With strong creative thinking supporting illustrations that work visually, the future can be so much brighter.

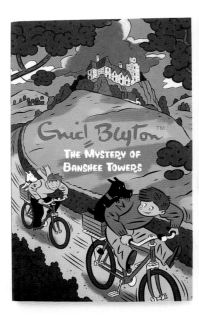

3.

4.

5.

6.

7.

A Life's Work – Jason Ford

1. Sketchbook study
Uncommissioned, 1990

2. Series of Children's Books
Egmont Books, 2003

3. Sketchbook study
Uncommissioned, 1995

4. Newspaper Supplement Cover
The Guardian, 1996

5. Newspaper Supplement Cover
The Independent, 2004

6. Newspaper Supplement Cover
The Guardian, 2000

7. Newspaper Supplement Cover
The Evening Standard, 1997

Jason Ford has worked as an illustrator since graduating from the Royal College of Art in London in 1989. Working initially in editorial publishing, Ford went on to expand his client base with commissions from book publishers, design companies and advertising agencies. The secret of Ford's success in building and maintaining such a fruitful career has been in the combination of both strength of thinking – the ideas and concepts within his work – aligned with the unique personality and flair in his drawing and execution.

1.

2.

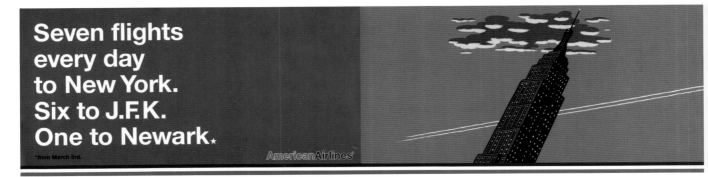

3.

Observer Wine page.   JasonFord '01

4.

A Life's Work – Jason Ford

1. Cassette case cover
BBC Worldwide Ltd, 2000

2. Promotional packaging
Vodafone, 2001

3. Billboard advertising campaign
American Airlines, 1998

4. Editorial commission
The Observer Wine Review, 2001

5. Agency promotion and exhibition
Art Directors Club of New York, 2003

6. Exhibition catalogue
Rogues Gallery, Pentagram, 2002

5.

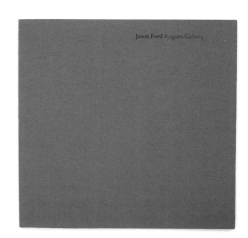

6.

2. THE MEDIUM IS THE MESSAGE

Illustrators communicate solely through their work; their subject matter and the strength of their ideas are vital aspects of the job. Less obvious, but as crucial, is the choice of medium, and use of materials is as essential as researching a subject and generating ideas and visual metaphors.

The Power of the Pencil

A common belief amongst graphic designers is that because the power of typography is entrusted to them alone, they hold all of the cards in the game of commercial design for print and screen. A little-known, or perhaps just rarely commented-upon fact that matches or even surpasses the claim to type by the designer is that the illustrator commands the power of the pencil. The pencil, and with it the activity of drawing in its broadest sense, is what defines the practice of illustration today.

It is hard to believe, but drawing can be a controversial subject. From the start of the journey from school pupil to art student and on to fully paid-up member of the illustration community, the practice of drawing can cause heated debate amongst practitioners. Art school teaching may seem radically different to students from the way in which they had been 'taught' previously. The use of new terminology also reflects a new stance and approach to this complex subject that may feel alien at first. The new vocabulary introduces phrases such as 'interpretative mark marking', 'intuitive and observational drawing of the figure', and 'exploring negative space'. For the first time, students may be encouraged to 'work back into a drawing with charcoal'. The essence of this approach to 'image-making' is to encourage experiment, rather than just training students in observational skills. This approach has typified the teaching of the subject since the 1950s and '60s.

The teaching of drawing will vary from art school to art school and may be influenced by fashions and movements in art and design. Although it might appear that artists and illustrators both approach the discipline from similar positions, the reality is somewhat different. Opinions are divided on the purpose of practice.

Generally, however, artists work to a self-set agenda, whilst illustrators start from a client-written brief. The artist may create work as part of the journey to the final solution, whilst the illustrator will produce work that ultimately sits within another context; that of the printed magazine or book jacket, reproduced from the original.

Drawing can be used for recording, representing and portraying. It can be observational or interpretative, can reflect a mood or a moment, or be utilised to purely convey information. Drawing is a hugely broad discipline and in the context of illustration, in the hands of illustrators, it is pushed to its very limits.

1.

2.

2. Coloured pencil on paper
'Bunting'
Andrew Brandou, 2004

3. Coloured pencil on paper
'Skunk'
Andrew Brandou, 2004

Bringing colour into a pencil-drawn illustration can be as straightforward as working with a range of coloured pencils. Although a traditional technique, it requires a unique understanding of the medium, built up through many years of practice.

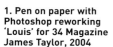
3.

1. Pen on paper with
Photoshop reworking
'Louis' for 34 Magazine
James Taylor, 2004

The simplest, yet most unforgiving medium is the pencil. There is very little room for error – an illustration rests on the artist's skills and ability. Photoshop may be used to clean and tidy up an image, but strong drawing techniques are the essence of the image.

1.

2.

From the start of the journey from school pupil to art student and on to fully paid-up member of the illustration community, the practice of drawing can cause heated debate amongst practitioners.

1. Biro pen on paper
'Vandal' for Nike
Billie-Jean, 2004

2. Biro pen on school desk
'Back to the Old School' for
Pentagram UK Exhibition
Billie-Jean, 2003

Some materials bring a certain substance to a project – the use of the ballpoint pen on lined paper evokes memories of doodling in school exercise books, whilst used to draw directly on to an old school desk, a real sense of the past is executed and recreated for an exhibition.

3.

4.

3. Pencil, pen and Adobe Streamline into vinyl graphic
In-store graphic for Carhartt
JAke, 2004

4. Pencil in sketchbook
Study for in-store graphic for Carhartt
JAke, 2004

Working sketches can form the basis of the final artwork for many projects – keeping the essence of spontaneity. Translating pencil-drawn images into larger wall or window graphics, for example, can be an interesting process. By taking original drawings into an application such as Streamline, converting into a vector line and then outputting on to vinyl, the image can then be adhered to a flat surface.

5.

5. Pen on paper
'You're Trying Too Hard'
Matt Sewell, 2005

Subtle use of colour can highlight key areas within the image. Knowing when and where it pays dividends to use colour sparingly comes with practice and experience – sometimes less is more.

1.

1. Pencil drawing
'Norsk Tales' for Smirnoff
Neal Murren, 2004

2. Digital colouring
'Norsk Tales' for Smirnoff
Neal Murren, 2004

Pencil drawings can also be
coloured entirely on-screen in
software applications such as Adobe
Photoshop, giving freedom and flexibility
to make changes and alterations
throughout the project.

2.

Material World

The job of the illustrator is relatively simple; the key to successful illustrating is in the essence of the message and the art of communication, as discussed in the previous chapter. It is, however, the medium or materials employed to convey that message that can assist in the correct reading and understanding. A strong idea visually translated using the most appropriate media, with excellent execution, will always lead to the most successful illustrative solutions.

With the apparent freedom of choice in medium that the illustrator has access to, comes a responsibility and understanding for the context in which they are to be applied and the historical or cultural nature of the materials and their usage in previous incarnations. There is little to be gained from illustrating mobile phone technology, for example, using an etching process. Working in a very linear way only in a vector application for an article about street market vendors would not demonstrate an affinity for the subject; the themes and messages would be distorted, and the medium might act as a barrier to the understanding of the message.

Equally, acknowledging historical and subject–specific references to materials ensures messages cannot be confused; why work in the flat, bold, primary-coloured comic style reminiscent of Roy Lichtenstein's Pop Art interpretations of comics for an illustration about the global ➡

3. Screenprint-inspired Photoshop collage
'Gaming' for New Scientist Magazine
Simon Pemberton, 2004

Taking inspiration from working methods such as screenprinting can provide a rich resource. Recreating analogue print techniques in digital formats saves time, resources and can make the impossible possible.

3.

stock markets? The perfect marriage of materials and message may sound like a cliché but makes real sense; after all, the mantra that 'form follows function' still holds a resonance today.

At the heart of all illustration, drawing plays a vital role. Without the ability to draw and visualise well the illustrator lacks the most important component in his or her toolbox. Illustrators have at their fingertips, literally in this increasingly digital age, tools that enable the creation of complex, layered, multifaceted images that can be created using a multitude of techniques, but without the power of the pencil, the illustrator may be as powerless as the designer that has failed to control typography.

1.

2.

**1. Digital collage
'Rabbit'
Michiko Tachimoto, 2004**

**2. Digital collage
'Tree'
Michiko Tachimoto, 2004**

Working in digital formats allows for the constant addition and subtraction of collage elements within a piece of work. Non-digital formats rarely allow for the constant moving of images in such a fully flexible fashion.

4.

5.

3.

**3. Digital drawing
'Bear and Hunter' for Sky+
Adrian Johnson, 2004**

**4. Digital drawing
'Darts' for Estates Gazette
Adrian Johnson, 2004**

**5. Digital drawing
'Robot' for The Guardian
Adrian Johnson, 2004**

Even when based on pencil drawings or
original layouts created in sketchbooks,
work that uses digital elements – be that
anything from vector lines or scanned
textures – is still classified as being done
entirely on-screen.

Celebrating Process

The process of creating images is a complex and personal journey for every individual illustrator. Often seemingly simple images can belie both the craft of the image-maker and the journey that the illustrator may have taken over previous years in order to reach a point where creating work becomes second-nature. Art school graduates of illustration courses often expect an instant flow of commissions, but it can take numerous months and occasionally years in honing and fine-tuning work before an image-maker feels truly confident as an illustrator.

Much of the struggle towards professionalism can be about the materials and processes that the illustrator starts to excel in working with; understanding how to use particular media can take time and practice, but is vital in mastering the ability to illustrate effectively and therefore professionally.

Many illustrators have a favourite range of materials that they will choose to work with. For many, the blend and scope of their chosen materials, tools and techniques is what helps to define the work that they produce. Experimenting with techniques and ways of working can be more important than exploring the scope of drawing and image-making itself. There are illustrators that work using the most simple methods imaginable – using a pencil, pen or paintbrush mark – whilst there are others that build up complex layers utilising techniques in photography, vector-applications and scanned montages of 'found' imagery, often priding themselves with their ability to hide the processes from the viewer. It is the celebration of the process and the techniques employed that interest and drive this particular breed of illustrators.

1.

2.

Celebrating Process

1. 3D Constructed collage
'East' for an exhibition
Paul Burgess, 1995

2. Painting and collage
'Park 'n' Ride' for solo exhibition
Paul Burgess, 2004

Working with 3D elements and collaged elements can mean having to photograph final results for reproduction. Lighting a constructed 3D image correctly is as vital as reproducing the brush marks in a collage that uses a 'found' thrift-store painting.

3. Hand painting and digital collage
'Thinktank' for Tom Brown
Brian Cairns, 2003

4. Hand painting and digital collage
'You' for Tom Brown
Brian Cairns, 2003

5. Hand painting and digital collage
'Dog' for Ski Magazine
Brian Cairns, 2004

6. Hand painting and digital collage on T-shirt
'Trees = Air' for Howies
Brian Cairns, 2004

Using digital processes should not hinder immediate-looking results – using a mix of hand-drawn images with hand-rendered type, painted textures and photographs gives a sketch-book quality to an illustration.

3.

4.

5.

The Process

• Methods and ways of working can take many years to fine-tune and make unique to an individual illustrator.

• There is always the temptation to take creative short-cuts – it's better to invest the time and effort in creating a way of working that no one else is doing though.

• Finding materials and processes that 'click' is part of the journey that all professional illustrators must take in order to create truly unique images.

• Increasingly illustrators are employing a range of methods and techniques that cross the divide between both analogue and digital worlds.

6.

Art School Ethos

From that first life-drawing class in the studio to the induction session in the print-making workshop or the introductory class in the darkroom, it is clear that art school offers a wealth of new creative opportunities to the young artist or designer. Generally it is recognised in art and design education that students will study a one-year basic course in art and design before embarking upon a more specialised three-year program in their chosen field. In the UK and Europe this general foundation course has often sat outside of the degree programme, but recently there has been an enthusiasm to adopt the model used in the USA, where the first year of art and design education is subsumed into the degree, effectively offering a four-year programme.

Maintaining the flavour of the foundation course will be important as this happens, as it is here that students are first introduced to new ways of working and thinking. Programmes of study allow students to briefly experience numerous disciplines within the broad spread of art and design, enabling them to decide what to study at degree level. Students then study alongside those that may have chosen to practice architecture, fashion, ceramics or automotive design for

1.

2.

3.

It is the division of disciplines and the creation of walled subject areas that helps to stamp out new, forward-thinking and possibly radical approaches to practice.

example, and it is in this mix of interests that many find inspiration for their work. Perhaps as important as the opportunity for practice, a strong art and design foundation course offers study, reflection and debate on art and design history, communication theories, politics and issues of race and gender.

This vital middle year of study, will, for many, be the only genuine opportunity for students from a variety of disciplines to discuss and debate issues. As students migrate towards their more subject-specific courses in the following year, they inevitably find themselves surrounded by others with similar interests and goals. For creative young artists and designers this can stifle debate and create unnecessary boundaries between disciplines that may never again be broken down. It is the division of disciplines and the creation of walled subject areas that helps to stamp out new, forward-thinking and possibly radical approaches to practice. Of course, questions will still be asked and debate will continue to rage, but only from within each of the divided subjects, and without external opinions and contributions much can remain unaltered and unchallenged.

4.

**1. Charcoal on paper
'Charlie Parker' for
Union Square Music
Chris Watson, 2004**

**2. Charcoal on paper
'Nat King Cole' for Union Square Music
Chris Watson, 2004**

**3. Charcoal on paper
'Billie Holiday' for Union Square Music
Chris Watson, 2004**

Traditional materials like charcoal require dextrous drawing skills. Images can be cleaned with the Eraser Tool in Photoshop in a more clinical way than a traditional putty rubber, but the drawing still relies on the artist's own techniques and ability.

**4. Acrylic paint on paper
'Solar System' for Private Commission
Luke Best, 2004**

**5. Acrylic paint on paper
'Unlucky in Love' for
Self-published Book
Luke Best, 2005**

A child-like drawing quality mixed with aspects of painting that echo 'Outsider' art that is rendered in simple, almost primary colours gives an other-worldly, naïve feel to an illustration – useful if it fits the subject being illustrated.

5.

The Use of Odd Media

Using paint straight out of the tube is frowned upon by the serious artist who feels it is important to mix the desired colour oneself rather than relying on the manufacturer to create the very hue needed. This may sound pompous or exaggerated, but the importance of the right materials for the artist should never be underestimated.

For some the allure of the art store and its contents is never enough and the route to creating truly original art is in re-appropriating existing or 'found' objects. Some illustrators create images from collaged elements, mixing and layering in both analogue and digital formats to create new variants.

Collage is not a new art form, it originally came to prominence with the birth of photography, but appears to have been given a new lease of life by digital technology. Originally created by graphic designers, the first to master the Mac in the late 1980s, collaged illustrations were created in applications such as Adobe Photoshop. Within a few years the illustrator had gained on lost ground and the range of illustrative expertise in the field of collage began to expand.

Making pictures from more challenging materials has interested illustrators wanting to ensure that their work is considered original. Using cut and torn coloured paper in the style of Henri Matisse or creating 'Box Art' in the manner of Joseph Cornell has attracted some illustrators away from traditional techniques, whilst others strive to use objects and items previously unused as art materials.

Illustrations created from coloured push pins set into a squared grid, or from cut and painted sheets of tin, or entirely collaged from tiny slivers of banknotes have all appeared in publications. The range of experimentation and sophistication employed across these untried and untested applications sets illustrators apart from others in the design profession; if a material has artistic potential, there is an illustrator ready to master it.

1.

The Use of Odd Media

**1. Drilled holes into MDF board
'Samuel Beckett' for group exhibition
Will Tomlinson, 2004**

Creating an image using light and shade by drilling holes of differing depths according to a pre-set pattern gives a new vision to a photographic portrait of Samuel Beckett. Although this image appears to have used digital processes at the end of its creation, in measuring the holes, this wasn't the case. A photo of Beckett was just digitally scanned at the beginning and reduced to just a few monochrome tones in Photoshop.

**2. Paper 'stick-up'
'San Juan' for personal project
Swoon, 2004**

Scale can give a new look to an existing image – printing on numerous paper panels and sticking to a flat surface eliminates any butting up or overlaying of sheets if exercised carefully.

**3 & 4. Mascara sticks on board
'Mask-era of Revolution'
Ian Wright, 2003**

Using 'found', but relevant objects to create an image provides interesting results – attempting to self-restrict a palette of colours or materials can force the illustrator into making more creative use of what is available.

2.

3.

*Making pictures from
more challenging materials
has always interested
illustrators wanting to
ensure that their work
is considered original.*

4.

The Use of Odd Media (II)

1. Hand-cut paper
'Shine Like a Star' series for
personal project
Pinky, 2005

Building layers of colour utilising a similar method to the way in which a screenprint is created, but using hand-cut coloured papers allows detail to show through in a unique and varied way.

Using Odd Media

• Being creative with media and processes means being able to find methods of creating images with materials that may not normally be used.

• Look for ways of working that differ from the norm – be experimental, but try to use media that relate to the subject that you are illustrating.

• It may be wise to have your final piece professionally photographed if the image is to be reproduced – getting lighting techniques to work correctly can be impossible without the right equipment.

• Be prepared for numerous attempts when mastering new or untried working methods – remember: new work takes time and patience.

1.

Illustration as a Discipline

As for boundaries and borderlines, it is clear that illustration sits somewhere between art and design. Never truly considered to be an adjunct of art with a capital 'A', nor wholly allowed to exist as a solo design discipline, without the prop that is graphic design, illustration has been continually disowned by both artists and designers. It has been derided as whimsical by the artist and 'arty' by the designer.

Outside of education there appears to be a blanket refusal by artists to acknowledge the importance of the role that illustration plays. The crossover from art to illustration is occasionally deemed appropriate, but the reverse is rarely accepted. In the design world, designers plunder freely from the fields of illustration, yet rarely take any responsibility for sowing new seeds, and little time or space is given to nurturing growth and emerging talent. It is interesting to note that the UK's foremost monthly design publication, Creative Review, dropped illustration as a category in its annual design awards; evidence of the lack of stature that the design community places on the role of illustration and the career of the illustrator.

➡

2. Marker pen and paint on metal construction 'Garbage Heads' Series for personal project Akira Wakui – 2004

3. Ink on paper 'Garbage Heads' Series for personal project Akira Wakui, 2004

Working from small-scale original drawings made with ink on paper, these larger metal constructions are hand-crafted before being hand-painted with drawn elements added prior to installation within a gallery environment.

3.

2.

Back in education, the discipline rarely fares any better; few institutions offer full-time courses purely in illustration, and those that do, offer very little by way of stand alone facilities. Illustration courses often do not occupy their own physical space, but sit in studios as part of graphic design courses. It is still the case that in many countries across Europe, illustration has failed to be recognised as a discipline and therefore courses tend not to exist at all. Professionally, illustrations for press and advertising have been created by designers and artists, and with no real recognition for the practice, the development of courses has remained as an off-shoot of graphic design, if at all.

Of course it is true that crossover and discussion can be nurtured across the two disciplines of graphic design and illustration. But this is only possible if both are given equal status and sadly, this is still a rare occurrence. With a high demand for facilities and studio space for courses requiring specialist equipment such as looms in textiles, kilns in ceramics, wood, metal and plastics, workshops in 3D design and black-and-white and digital darkrooms in photography, it is clear – although unjustified – why illustration often remains at the end of the list.

1.

1. Paint on board
'Wasted' for 2M
Louise Weir, 2003

2. Paint on board
'Flesh and Bone' for 2M
Louise Weir, 2003

3. Paint on board
'Safe as Houses' for 2M
Louise Weir, 2003

Traditional techniques such as painting have started to have more impact in recent years. With so many illustrators having gone over to digital working methods, older, more established ways of image-creation have become more sought after.

3.

2.

Outside of education there appears to be a
blanket refusal by artists to acknowledge the
importance of the role that illustration plays.
The crossover from art to illustration is
occasionally deemed appropriate, but
the reverse is rarely accepted.

A Demanding Life

Illustration is not for the faint-hearted. It can take a tough cookie to meet the demands and rigours of getting somewhere within a discipline that feels vastly unsupported. Without stand alone facilities in education, the lone illustrator must utilise the media that other disciplines would first lay claim to, breaking into places that would normally be considered the domain of other specialists. Gaining access to the drawing studio normally housed in the fine art department, the darkrooms occupied by the photography course, the print-making workshops open for students of print-making, the wood and metal workshops utilised by students of sculpture, architecture and furniture design and the computing facilities overrun by graphic design and motion graphics students is never going to be easy. But it happens – illustration students are a rare breed that open doors and get things moving.

A life without a defined career path is not for all: creating and then maintaining a presence as an illustrator within the design industry takes commitment and at times can be frustrating. Dragging a portfolio of work to a potential client to find that they have left the building is depressing, and being at the mercy of those with the power to commission can be demoralising, but at the heart of those that wish to work in illustration is the desire to create images.

Working with new materials, solving visual problems, researching subjects and experimenting with ideas, all drive most illustrators. Seen by many as a lifestyle rather than just a career choice, the commitment to the discipline must be all-encompassing if a student illustrator is to break into the commercial world. Never likely to be a regular nine-to-five existence with healthcare, dental and paid holidays, illustration demands total involvement. Working across the board, breaking across boundaries, experimenting and mastering media, none truly belonging to them, the illustrator still finds ways of making his or her mark.

1. Screen-printed T-shirt
'Untitled' for Concrete Hermit
Jon Burgerman, 2004

2. Digital drawing
'Phalanx' for Uberhaus
Jon Burgerman, 2004

3. Hand-drawn customised guitar
'Guitar' for Studio Output
Jon Burgerman, 2004
Art Direction by Studio Output

4. Hand-drawn customised shoes
'Untitled' for Sneaker Pimps
Jon Burgerman, 2004

Having an appetite for working across a broad spectrum of applications is a huge motivation for approaching clients with ideas of how various techniques may work. Images that work on paper in print may also work on T-shirts and can be adapted for a 3D object like a guitar or a pair of sneakers.

1.

2.

5.

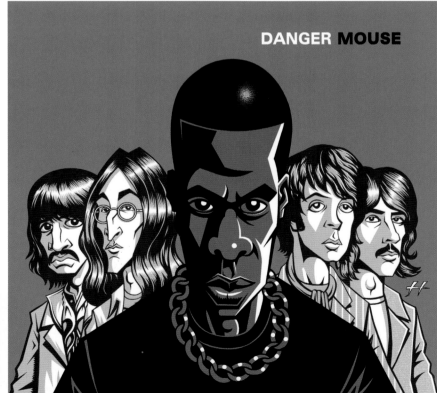

6.

4.

5. Screen-printed poster
'Beastie Boys' for Monqui Presents
Justin Hampton, 2004

6. Screen-printed poster
'Dangermouse' for Dangermouse
Justin Hampton, 2004

Some media live on despite the allure of
the digital. Screen-printed posters have
a quality that is unique and cannot be
replicated by digital print processes.

3.

Mixing Media

Without the confines of a discipline-specific medium, the illustrator has been free to explore and experiment with a range of media, creating images from whatever and wherever seems most appropriate. With drawing at the centre of the illustrator's armoury, the handmade mark is never far from view, but unsurprisingly it is the vast range of potential image and mark-making devices that appears in the work of, and typifies the eclectic nature of, today's image-makers.

Like professional magpies, illustrators plunder an array of media, employing working methods that mix and match depending on the requirements of the project. It is not uncommon to witness a raw visual mix of the digital, the analogue, the traditional, the photographic and the stencilled, as well as hand-drawn and painted marks within the images of contemporary illustrators. The digital has empowered the illustrator in a way that was thought unthinkable even just a decade and a half ago.

1.

4.

1. Digital drawing and digital
   photographic composite
   'Sore Leg' for NHS
   Andrew Rae, 2004

2. Digital drawing and digital
   photographic composite
   'Stairs' for NHS
   Andrew Rae, 2004

3. Digital drawing and digital
   photographic composite
   'Bike Crash' for NHS
   Andrew Rae, 2004

4. Digital drawing and digital
   photographic composite
   'Monkey Dust' for BBC
   Andrew Rae, 2004

Combining hand-rendered, digitally-
drawn characters with real digitally-shot
backgrounds gives an image a realistic yet
edgy feel. Equally effective can be the
dropping in of a photographic sky to a
hand-drawn and coloured illustration.

2.

3.

The Digital Divide

The graphic designer, as well as keeping a tight rein on the ownership of typography, was also able to maintain control of the digital process for quite some time too. Eager to explore the extent that these digital processes had to offer, graphic designers were quick to leap on the new wave in design technology afforded by the computer when Apple launched the Macintosh in 1984. Billed as the alternative to IBM, the Mac was the first personal computer with a graphic interface and was to revolutionise the way that people used computers. Leapt upon by innovators in the design industry, the $2500 price tag gave the user just 128KB of RAM, but nonetheless, the digital age for the designer had begun.

In-house Investment...

Left out in the cold, most illustrators were unable to match the financial power that designers could call upon. Crucially it would be straightforward economics that would hold illustration back by almost ten years from partaking in the digital design revolution. The graphic designer working for a graphic design company could be in front of a computer without any personal financial outlay. Undertaking training courses and getting up to speed with the necessary software applications, although still creatively and technically in their infancy, could also be fairly easily accomplished by the employee of even a mid-sized design company. It was good business sense for a company to buy computers and train designers accordingly.

...v. Small Freelance Budgets

For illustration the situation was somewhat different. For illustrators, to work in an independent freelance capacity simply meant that the purchase of digital hardware would be out of reach for sometime. The price of software was prohibitively expensive and so costs needed to fall dramatically before the tide would turn. As well as a reduction in hardware and software costs, it would also take the expertise of those designers and art directors commissioning illustration to have a knowledge of working practice in digital reproduction and print processes before the barriers would eventually fall down. It was the turn of the century before digital processes finally made their mark on the practice of illustration.

1.

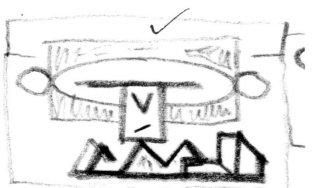

2.

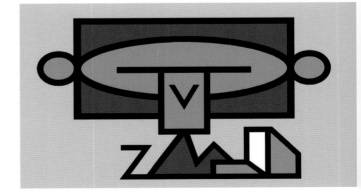

3.

1. Digital drawing
'Une, Deux, Trois' for
Teachers Magazine
Matt Pattinson, 2005

2. Pencil compositional sketch
'Mon Key' for personal project
Matt Pattinson, 2005

3. Digital drawing
'Mon Key' for personal project
Matt Pattinson, 2005

Even the simplest of images that can
be created in moments on a computer
can take hours of concentrated work
to produce using analogue techniques.

4. Digital drawing
'Hoxton Apocalypse' for 333
Elliot Thoburn, 2004

Digital techniques allow
constant repositioning of elements
within an illustration as well as
constant recolouring and retouching. The
final artwork can always be
altered – and so not nearly as final
as the terminology suggests.

*Crucially, it would be
straightforward economics
that would hold illustration
back by almost ten years
from partaking in the
digital design revolution.*

4.

Using the Computer

No one tool or process has had as much influence on the methods employed by the illustrator as the computer. If it is the pencil that wields the power, then it is the computer that harnesses that power and enables the illustrator to transform the pencil mark into a seemingly never-ending array of new marks. The rebirth and re-interest in the craft of illustration can be attributed directly to the role that the computer has played.

The computer has helped to place illustration on a level with other disciplines, and the range of digital possibilities – coupled with the technical power now found within the reach of most illustrators has ensured a more equal relationship with design. Illustrators, with the aid of digital processes, are returning to the roots of the practice. Illustration first grew from a branch of graphic design that was commercial art, and now increased involvement with projects and commissions during the design stage has begun to echo that early approach as illustrators increasingly work across the board.

Creating artwork that was 'camera ready' became the only technical requirement for illustrators in the years leading to the digital revolution; as many were working less in design studios and more and more from their own studios and homes, it was easy for designers to keep them out of the loop when it came to making design decisions about projects. Digital technology started to change the input that illustrators would have, allowing opportunities for discussion and debate about reproduction issues, print processes and paper stocks, as well as entirely digital outlets for illustration such as the Web and television. Contributing to these changes in practice were both the power and knowledge, digital illustrators now had access to and the ease of communication afforded by email and mobile phone technology. From their own freelance workspace illustrators could work alongside designers with communication lines open at all times.

A relationship built on trust began to evolve slowly as illustrators started to emerge from the dawn of their own digital age – albeit ten years after the desk-top revolution had re-energised graphic design – with portfolios of work that impressed a younger more streetwise design community. Constantly looking for new ways of expressing ideas and communicating to their clients, graphic design saw a fresh approach to image-making in digital illustration. Impressed with the ability to harness both absolute skills in drawing and image manipulation alongside the vast array of possibilities that the digital opened up, graphic design began to recognise the importance of illustration within the design process.

1.

2.

1. spencer wilson / illustrator   © 2005

phone 0793 263 6845 or email spencer@spencerwilson.co.uk
further examples of work can be found at www.spencerwilson.co.uk and www.peepshow.org.uk

WWW.
SPENCER
WILSON
.CO.UK

3.

Digital Illustration

1. Original pencil visual
Satoshi Matsuzawa, 2004

2. Vector-drawn digital Image
Satoshi Matsuzawa, 2004

Many illustrators that work to create
entirely digital artwork will start with
a pencil rough or visual. Scanned into
a vector application such as Adobe
Illustrator and used a guide to 'trace'
or re-draw the image – the layer is then
removed at the end of the process.

3. Vector-drawn digital image
Self-promotion mailer
Spencer Wilson, 2005

4. Vector-drawn digital image
'Ebay' for The Daily Telegraph
Newspaper
Spencer Wilson, 2005

Mastering a vector application so that
the software works as intuitively as
the pencil is key to creating unique
illustrations that allow the content
to rise above the styling.

4.

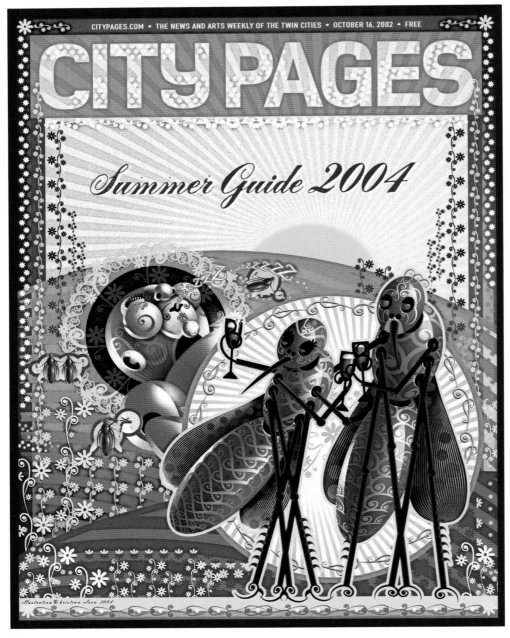

1.

Digital Illustration (II)

1. Digital drawing and digital collage composite
'Summer' For City Pages
Kristian Olson, 2004

There are techniques employed by many illustrators that could not easily have been created without the aid of digital technology. Previously, images such as these would have only been possible through intense hand-rendered workmanship and almost certainly not in the timescale that most commissions dictate.

2 & 3. Digital drawing
'Sex' series for Eastpress
Izumi Nogawa, 2004

Digital illustration has demonstrated that it can offer creative communication solutions that photography can't compete with in terms of both price and speed of turnaround.

Leapt upon by innovators in the design industry, the $2500 price tag gave the user just 128KB of RAM, but nonetheless the digital age for the designer had begun.

2.

3.

Digital Timeline

• 1970
Ken Thompson and Dennis Ritchie build the UNIX operating system.

• 1971
Intel creates the first single-chip microprocessor – the 4-bit Intel 4004.

• 1973
IBM creates the first true sealed hard disk drive.

• 1975
The MITS Altair is the first personal computer to warrant serious attention at a cost of only $439.00.

• 1977
The Apple 11 debuts at the first West Coast Computer Fair in San Francisco.

• 1977
Bill Gates and Paul Allen start Microsoft in New Mexico.

• 1981
IBM launch the first PC, based on an open architecture and license DOS from a tiny company called Microsoft.

• 1981
The Xerox Alto introduces the graphical user interface along with the mouse, the desktop metaphor, icons, windows and menus.

• 1982
Commodore introduces the first truly price-friendly computer at $400.00 and 22 million are sold.

• 1984
In January Apple launches the first Macintosh, with its graphical user interface, creating a bigger stir than the IBM PC did in 1981.

• 1985
The Commodore Amiga debuts with advanced graphics and sound combined with a multitask operating system and graphical user system.

• 1985
Windows appears for the first time, before going through numerous updates and changes.

• 1986
The Intel 80386 Processor chips, bringing in a 32-bit architecture and capable of breaking the 640KB memory barrier, as well as running software written for graphical interfaces.

• 1987
Apple launch the first colour Macintosh, the Mac 11, able to display 256 colours at a time from a palette of 16 million.

• 1990
Adobe launch Photoshop. It goes on to dominate the photo editing market.

• 1991–92
New formats evolve including QuickTime from Apple, as well as the JPEG and MPEG formats for saving and viewing files. Kodak launch the Photo CD at this time too.

• 1994
Apple Power Mac introduced and within a year over a million are sold. A basic machine with 8MB of RAM, 250MB hard disk, a CD-ROM drive and a 14" colour monitor came in at $2289.

• 1994
The WWW revolution gets fully underway as the number of hosts hit two million and the number of websites reaches 600.

• 1995
MP3 is developed and accepted as the standard compression platform for storing music digitally.

• 1997
DVD technology announced and within a few years can be played and recorded on personal computers.

• 1998
Apple launch the iMac based on the G3 chip launched in the professional range the year before.

• 2001
Apple launch a range of G4 Powerbooks that revolutionises how illustrators work.

• 2003
Adobe launch Creative Suite – a professional integrated software package comprising of Photoshop, Illustrator and InDesign.

The New Wave of Illustrators

Interestingly, a revolution was taking place away from the confines of professional illustration and the often-stifling demands of commercial work. The uprising was subtle and not started on the battlegrounds familiar to the old guard of illustrators. A new wave was honing its skills away from regular illustration outlets, producing work that refused to pander to the art directors of glossy monthly magazines or the Sunday supplements. Away from the scrutiny of the design press, from organisations such as The Society of Illustrators in New York and The Association of Illustrators in London, and away also from the watchful eyes of the illustration agencies struggling to keep afloat during the rigours of the industry recession. The tide was turning.

The new wave of illustrators with a new approach, with something to say and the ways and means of saying it, started to command control. No longer indulging the needs of dull business-to-business corporate clients, a savvier, more fashion-conscious, streetwise illustrator had started to create images for an audience made up of its own peers. Independent magazines and record labels, the established 'style' press, as well as small fashion companies started to employ the services of this new breed.

The following two moments are now recognised as key in the rebirth of illustration. In the UK The Face magazine employed an illustrator as art director and the look and feel of the magazine changed almost overnight. Funky, quirky and urban images by new illustrators started to appear and the ratio of illustration to photography was healthier than ever before. In the US, Levi's were quick to capture the new mood and commissioned illustrators to create ad campaigns and illustrate their urban clothing ranges, breaking the mould and allowing illustration to depict fashion in a way that had been the proviso of the photographer. Keen to capture the zeitgeist and stay ahead of the pack, this new and increasing client list all took to 'new' illustration with open arms. But what had really changed within illustration?

1.

2.

The revolution had occurred for a number of reasons; the first was the age of the average new image-maker. Younger but already with an established grip on taming the technology, probably due to an earlier introduction to the computer than any other generation before, this new breed felt empowered rather than hindered. Just one generation of illustrator before – generations appearing to change every five years within the discipline – and much had remained static. Not tied down with the baggage of time, nor attempting to pacify the old guard or fit into an existing order, allowed the renegades of 'new' illustration the freedom to experiment.

Another reason for change stemmed from what really excited these fresh illustrators; the scope now offered by the mix of digital and analogue techniques. Introduced to a vast range of techniques and media during their first foundation course at art school and able to refine their skills throughout the nomadic existence that typified degree-level teaching of illustration, an enthusiasm had grown for what they considered 'new' technology; traditional techniques and methods. The eclectic nature of their image-making skills was to be matched only by the eclectic nature of the subjects and themes covered and explored by these new illustrators. Often those setting their own parameters and goals, and investigating themes and issues of a personal nature has led to spin-off projects with real fees. Others, working like designers, have gone out to meet with potential clients directly, instigating projects that they have an affinity for.

This shift in power has been another spin-off of the revolution.

The themes explored by this new wave are not new – many of them are already well-investigated and documented within editorial and fine art photography – but for illustration it was a much-needed shot in the arm. Not all of the new work appearing followed the age-old mantra that deemed that the best illustration must contain a great 'idea'; for many, it was more about the look and feel, the mood or essence, than the communication of a 'clever' idea. Gritty urban backdrops vie for attention with drawings of beautiful, yet often tragic-looking people, set against themes that include sex, music, and relationships; sometimes dark and surreal, sometimes humourous and playful. The strand that holds this range of diverse subjects and picture-making skills together, is the belief in the importance of the creation of unique new visual worlds. Those illustrators that truly work within that space where art and design meet have reinvented and rejuvenated illustration, and underpinning the discipline has been the belief in the drawn mark and the power of the pencil, albeit with a digital twist.

A new wave was honing its skills away from regular illustration outlets, producing work that refused to pander to the art directors of glossy monthly magazines or the Sunday supplements.

1. Hand-rendered drawing and stencil with digital redrawing and retouching 'Deconstructing Kylie' for Kylie La La La by William Baker Miles Donovan, 2003

2. Hand-rendered stencil with digital redrawing, retouching and collage 'Access' for Wire Design Miles Donovan, 2004

Subversive, angry and with aspects of a punk DIY ethos, a new wave of illustrators emerged producing work with a stripped-down feel that utilised both analogue and digital working methods to full effect.

1.

1. Digital vector drawing 'Cornershopcornucpiarama' for Marmalade Magazine
Mr Bingo, 2004

2. Digital vector drawing 'These Arms' for Oxfam
Mr Bingo, 2005

Much of the subject matter being tackled by this new breed of illustrator offered opportunities to create work of a humorous and playful nature, as well as hard-hitting campaigns of a graphic nature.

2.

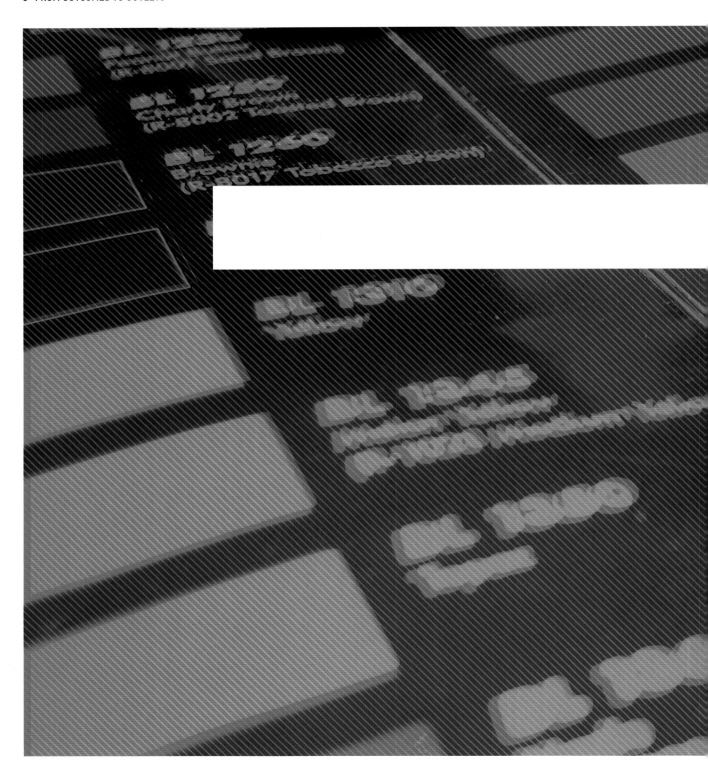

3. FROM OUTCOMES TO OUTLETS

It is one thing to master the art of illustration from the comfort of the art school studio or the warmth of the back bedroom, but working to commission faced with a real brief, a real client and a real deadline is an entirely different process. Different sectors of the design, advertising and publishing worlds each have their own complexities and demands.

The Overview

The illustrator's business landscape of design, advertising and publishing has undergone enormous change during the past few decades. The role that graphic communication plays in our everyday lives, here at the start of the 21st century, has never been more intense, complex and demanding for the viewer.

In this increasingly digital age, visual communication must compete fiercely for our attention and we stand in the firing line. Free magazines are thrust at us as we leave railway stations, we are handed club flyers on every other urban street corner and we are broadcast to 24 hours a day, 365 days of the year, by a seemingly endless supply of TV channels. The Sunday (and increasingly Saturday) newspapers require us to have put in time at the gym if we plan on walking home from the newsagent.

We are fired at by promos, advertorials and infomercials. We are spammed, texted and blogged. Visual communication is on-line, on-screen, downloadable and upgradeable. Never before have we been so bombarded from every quarter, so image-saturated, manically marketed to and media-manipulated. And we only have ourselves to blame for this situation as the media feeds an insatiable thirst from a knowledge-hungry public: we ceaselessly demand the latest, the newest and the best, devouring information at a truly astonishing rate with no let-up from the avalanche that we have created.

Illustration has the power to capture a personality, a point of view.

1.

1. Fortnightly Magazine
MacUser
'The Acceleration Game'
Richard May, 2003

2. Weekly Magazine
Time Out
'The Washington Sniper'
Richard May, 2003

A bold and stylish use of illustration running full-bleed (over the page edges) across an entire double page spread differentiates an article on Apple Macintosh processor speeds from the predominance of photographic-led imagery in the rest of this issue of MacUser magazine. This technique is also employed by Time Out magazine – in both cases the text of the articles is incorporated into the illustration, either printed over in black or reversed out in white.

2.

To even compete in this cut-throat communication war, those companies that seek to differentiate their products and publications have started to understand that creating a brand awareness which offers a unique vision or visual can, in turn, offer some small measure of individualism in this crowded marketplace. Illustration has thus found favour once again, not just because interesting, sassy work is in evidence, but because it is the key to creating images that reflect more than just photographic evidence. Illustration has the power to capture a personality, a point of view. It can encapsulate a mood or a moment, and can tell a story to give a product history, depth and meaning.

Illustration and Graphic Design

However powerful illustration as a form of communication is, without graphic design, it would struggle to exist. Graphic design communicates, persuades, informs and educates. It covers a vast array of commercial applications and in trying to visualise the scope and breadth of the discipline it is wise to remember that all communication design has emerged from is practice.

The street sign, the book or newspaper, the CD sleeve, the instructions on the medicine bottle, the pack that contains your favourite brand of breakfast cereal or the software that you use have all been touched by the hand of the graphic designer.

The design studio sits at the heart of commercial graphics and these companies or departments of bigger organisations work across the various diverse sectors of the industry.

The scope of work for design companies and studios can be endless and it is here that the working relationship with graphic design starts for the illustrator. Understanding how the industry operates and the numerous sectors function is fundamental to ensuring that the relationship with graphic design can be most fruitfully exploited.

Editorial Illustration

Editorial work is a fundamental aspect of the job of illustration, and it is often bread-and-butter work for most professionals. With an ever-increasing range of daily and monthly magazines catering to general, specific and niche markets, this is a rich vein for an illustrator to mine.

Using illustration makes real sense for the editor of a newspaper supplement or magazine. With photography used to present an image as fact, illustration can be applied to features to indicate a personal viewpoint or an idea. It is the contrast that illustration offers to photography that works so well in editorial projects and it is rare to find illustration used outside of this in a publishing context.

Due to massive increases in the number and circulation of newspapers and magazines, and the knock-on increase in feature or opinion-driven articles, there is a plethora of commissions available every month. Add to the stock available in most newsagents and book stores the huge number of in-house magazines produced for insurance companies, banks, airlines, retail outlets and others, and the number of potential commissions grows accordingly. Illustrators working successfully in this huge sector can keep themselves very busy.

In editorial illustration budgets can be tight and it is important for the professional to maintain a steady flow of work and to ensure invoices are issued on a regular basis. Despite the relatively low fees, most illustrators still enjoy the creative freedom of working for newspapers and magazines; being left to be inventive and original are the rewards here. The freedom to develop new working methods within a project, showcase skills and test new ideas without excessive art direction from an art director or editor can

be invaluable. For those illustrators given a regular 'slot' in a weekly or monthly magazine, the challenge of developing fresh ideas for the same subject on a regular basis can be enjoyably stimulating.

Art Direction

Understanding how illustrators are commissioned is key to successful working relationships but despite that, few art and design courses truly replicate the procedure. Whilst there are relatively few courses in illustration compared to those teaching straight graphic design, there are even fewer that teach how to art direct. Most courses offer it, if at all, as part of their graphic design programme, without recognising the breadth of the discipline. This is also true for advertising art direction, therefore many art directors have to learn on the job; some manage brilliantly, others not so well.

The approach to commissioning illustration for a newspaper or magazine art department is often dictated by the deadline, which is sometimes just a few days from the initial point of contact and/or briefing. There is scant time for meeting illustrators in the flesh when commissioning and the typical briefing is often far short of ideal.

Art directors or art editors normally call an illustrator directly, as many are unwilling to work with illustration agencies. Agents exist to represent the interests of the illustrator and will often attempt to increase a fee, however, in editorial work there is very little, if any, room for manoeuvre. Art directors rarely want this associated inconvenience, as there is little time for negotiation with a deadline approaching. Deadlines in editorial work are unforgiving; few other areas of the discipline work as rapidly.

The Brief

Much can happen between the initial brief to the finished artwork. A good art director will, at the point of offering the work, have a brief or some copy to hand and be able to talk through the project. A brief may take different formats, but should include

1.

2.

3.

**1 & 2. Weekly newspaper magazine
The Guardian Weekend
'Karma Comedian'
Ray Smith, 2003**

**3. Weekly newspaper magazine
The Guardian Weekend
'Yesterday'
Ray Smith, 2003**

Illustrations that incorporate a technique utilising digital redrawn, reworked and collaged photographic elements are used to great effect across a full single page and through the gutter (the centre) for a newspaper's weekly colour magazine supplement. Creating striking, well-executed and forward-thinking illustrations to a strict deadline, an even stricter budget, often without the full text supplied, is all part of working as an editorial illustrator.

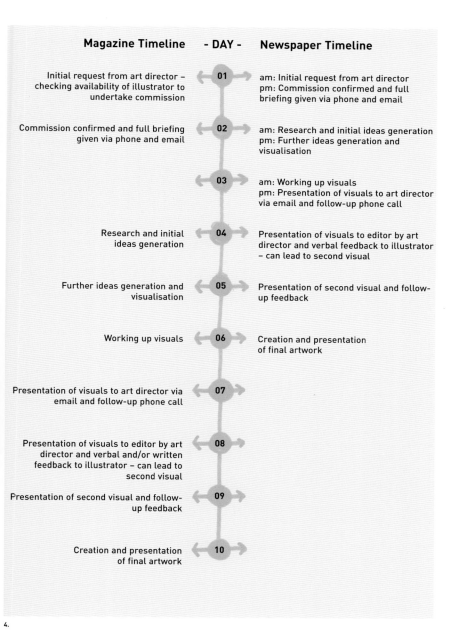

Magazine Timeline	- DAY -	Newspaper Timeline
Initial request from art director – checking availability of illustrator to undertake commission	01	am: Initial request from art director pm: Commission confirmed and full briefing given via phone and email
Commission confirmed and full briefing given via phone and email	02	am: Research and initial ideas generation pm: Further ideas generation and visualisation
	03	am: Working up visuals pm: Presentation of visuals to art director via email and follow-up phone call
Research and initial ideas generation	04	Presentation of visuals to editor by art director and verbal feedback to illustrator – can lead to second visual
Further ideas generation and visualisation	05	Presentation of second visual and follow-up feedback
Working up visuals	06	Creation and presentation of final artwork
Presentation of visuals to art director via email and follow-up phone call	07	
Presentation of visuals to editor by art director and verbal and/or written feedback to illustrator – can lead to second visual	08	
Presentation of second visual and follow-up feedback	09	
Creation and presentation of final artwork	10	

4.

4. Timeline for editorial commissions

The production schedule for all editorial commissions can be demanding. This is especially so for daily and weekly newspapers. Production deadlines are immovable – a newspaper must be delivered on time. Working in this field can be rewarding creatively, if not financially.

the following in addition to the text to be illustrated: the size the image will run in publication, the fee, and the deadline. Less key, but still important, is knowing on which side of the page the illustration will fall. Whether it sits on the left or right page of the spread can influence how an image is constructed; a figure, for example, can be either positioned entering or exiting the publication.

In reality, the art director may have to wait for copy from the editor, cutting down the time the illustrator has to work on ideas and final artwork. With most illustrators now working with access to broadband or at least dial-up Internet access, the text usually arrives via email. A brief for an editorial commission is likely to be little more than an early version of the copy that can be subject to change and the illustrator may need to actively request the other details of the project. Requesting all information, including the fee and the deadline, must be undertaken before embarking on the project; if in doubt, ask the relevant questions.

Once underway, a commission usually involves two stages; creating a rough version, referred to as a sketch or visual, and then the final artwork. All illustrators have different approaches to how they start a job, but all agree that reading, digesting and understanding the brief is crucial. Before embarking on the illustration, the first step is to understand the publication. Read previous copies to gauge the profile, look at who it is aimed at and research the title. Discuss with the art director why you have been chosen for the job, and ask if there was a particular piece of work or publicity that prompted the call. It is not unusual for a piece of previously printed publicity to be still working on your behalf five years later, are you still working in this particular way? It is wise to check before creating an illustration that is unlike the vision that the art director has of your work.

Art directors can have very distinct ideas of how they expect the copy to be visualised, while others allow for an open interpretation by the illustrator. Keeping the art director informed will help ensure that there are no difficulties later in the project. Even if you intend to work on the project later in the day or week, read the brief immediately upon receipt. Do this to consider ideas, visual representations and overall elements that may appear in the illustration. Having the subject of the brief in the mind will be conducive to contemplating solutions, and will highlight any potential problems early in the process.

➡

Research

Much of the enjoyment and the challenge in working as an illustrator lies in understanding and comprehending the subject of the text, as well as solving its visual interpretation.

Illustrators find that within a relatively short period of time they have to become an expert in the subject they are illustrating. The article may be about human relationships, neurosurgery, green politics, inner-city housing issues, car airbag systems or legal changes for solicitors; possibilities are endless and flexibility in visualising a range of subjects will be the key to working for a variety of publications.

Further research of subjects for a greater knowledge and understanding is part of the process. An article intended for publication may assume specialist knowledge from its intended audience – a specialist knowledge that the illustrator may have to rapidly get up to speed with.

Stage One: Visuals

For illustrators working on editorial jobs, the first stage of creating visuals must come quickly. Start to visualise ideas through sketching, mapping, doodling and drawing. Record initial thoughts and ideas and make notes or lists as a useful starting point. Carrying a small notebook and pen or pencil will help as not all ideas and concepts come to those at their desks, they may start to formulate on the bus, in the supermarket or at the cinema.

Responding to the brief can take time, but this is in short supply in editorial commissions so most illustrators have mechanisms to aid the process. It may be as simple as turning a mobile phone off, putting the kettle on and making tea or listening to classical music. It is . important to ensure there is 'thinking time' in which to come up with ideas and start to visualise them.

Art directors understand that not all illustrators work alike; they recognise that just because one likes to produce very finished and polished visuals there are others who scribble their intentions haphazardly, offering just a vague intention of how they intend to proceed. However roughs or visuals are produced, it is beneficial to all involved in the commission if much of the detail is resolved at this early stage. Failing to communicate the intentions of how the illustration will be executed, both conceptually and artistically, can lead to greater problems further into the project. Emailing or faxing a visual to an art director gives them something solid to show the editor, normally the one with the final say in what is to be published.

A great idea only works if it communicates well and the visuals stage is the first real test of a concept and its validity. A good art director will view the visual through the eyes of the publication's readership to ensure that the image and concept will work. Building time into a project to allow for a rejection at the concept/visual stage is paramount; not all projects go according to the wishes of the illustrator.

Create more than one idea at the first stage; opt to show just your favourite solution first, holding the others in reserve or put forward all of your ideas and allow the art director to decide on the one that best communicates. Never create just one concept, you run the risk of the project falling apart if you have no alternatives to offer and work into final artwork before the deadline draws close.

Stage Two: Final Artwork

However arrived at, the point of executing the final artwork is another crucial aspect of any editorial job. Ensuring that the art director understands the method intended is important if you work in a number of different media. If a commission has arisen from a photographic technique, for example, a similar technique must be employed in the final artwork as opposed to a more drawn or painterly approach – unless specifically requested. Not many art directors will be aware of every method that an illustrator employs, again this is a positive reason for clear lines of communication at the outset of the project. Positive surprises are the only surprises that an art director takes kindly to on the day of the deadline.

The Editorial Illustrator

An Interview with Autumn Whitehurst

Editorial work for magazines and newspapers is the life-blood for many illustrators, allowing unique opportunities for showcasing new approaches and working methods. What is your take on this aspect of the industry and why is it important for you to participate in editorial illustration?

AW – Editorial work is generally an illustrator's playground. Though it doesn't pay anywhere nearly as much as advertising work does, I find it to be the place in which I evolve. The clients are less inclined to define your approach so it's a great opportunity to really push yourself into fresh territory. This is very important to me because I have less and less free time in which to do work that allows me to explore my creative options.

You appear to have a very labour-intensive working method, could you describe the process, both conceptually and practically, in making your work?

AW – The very first thing I do is lay out my sketches in Illustrator because it allows me to distort the elements until everything feels harmonious. The rendering work is done with Photoshop brushes, much like a painter would use paintbrushes, although painting digitally demands a different kind of precision due to the nature of the program. I then use photo references to help me understand how light wraps around the body, but beyond that it's up to my imagination, and much of my effort goes into making these figures long and sleek.

As far as concepts go, I respond to assignments with my intuition. If I have to think about it too hard, then I know that I've taken the wrong approach and that the illustration will be dead if I attempt to finish it. It's usually a particular kind of emotion that I'm after and the technique that I'm using lends itself to that. Highly narrative work is difficult to achieve because rendering the skin so heavily sets a kind of pace throughout the image that must be maintained. Even in an environment built up with line-work, everything needs to be very tight so it can be extremely time-consuming. This has been my motive for creating a second body of work that is simpler in its execution and this is what I'm slowly working towards.

Illustration can bring a different viewpoint from photography to a subject when used in a magazine. Your work sits quite firmly in the middle of these processes, at least in visual terms; how does that affect your interpretation of the brief/assignment?

"Editorial work is generally an illustrator's playground. Though it doesn't pay anywhere nearly as much as advertising work does, I find it to be the place in which I evolve."

AW – I have to consider what I'm committing myself to in the initial stages because of the time involved in rendering the flesh, but there is also the pleasure of being able to take it a step further to create something that is almost like a fantasy, and this is liberating. I was concerned for a while about how close to photography some of the images were becoming, and wondered if it defeated the purpose of using illustration to accomplish what I was trying to achieve, but a friend pointed out that retouching a photo to such a degree would involve a lot more time than I was investing and that made me feel better about it.

By their very nature, magazines – and particularly newspapers – are only in the public eye for a short space of time and they have to relate to fashions and trends in image-making. How do you maintain an awareness of current design trends and keep one step ahead of the competition?

AW – I can't deny how influential excellent work is in that it sets a standard I'd like to meet. I work the only way that I know how so I don't think much about trends. They seem a bit dangerous, because to follow them could end in career suicide once the industry decides to move on. It's very important to keep evolving my abilities and I find that this happens more so in the editorial work.

Please give a brief outline of your intentions when making illustrations for this sector of the industry?

AW – I just want to make something as beautiful as I can within the given deadline so as to grab the readers' attention. Most of the commissions that I've been receiving are somehow fashion-related, so at the moment I'm concerned with creating images that have sex appeal. I want them to really sing, to be compositionally solid and ideally to suck the reader into a space that feels like a dream.

THE GUILTY BRIDE

HOW CAN A GIRL RAISED TO STAND ON HER OWN TWO FEET LEARN TO STAND BY HER MAN? RACHAEL COMBE ON BECOMING A WIFE

s it so wrong to want a cake plate? What about matching cake pans, an electric hand mixer, and a double boiler? Is that, like, *wrong*? Once you have all that gear, is it so wrong to spend a whole afternoon baking a devil's food cake with marshmallow frosting that requires you to stand over the stove with the mixer on high speed, splattering boiling-hot corn syrup and egg whites all over your forearms? Is it wrong to then go out to three different stores to find the special little Cadbury chocolates that look like robins' eggs that they sell only at Easter and to arrange them in a flower pattern on top of your magnificent cake, which rests upon its sparkling pedestal? Is it wrong to then take pictures of the cake and spend a good five minutes just gazing at it, joyfully, reverently, imagining the delight of your dinner guests when they get a load of your magical, wondrous, unbelievable cake?

Because when I did this a few weeks ago and plopped it down on the table after dinner—voilà!—and my boyfriend, O., then announced that I'd made it from scratch, our guests just looked at me blankly for a moment before someone said, "Uh, since when did you become Southern?" Then they all laughed. I blushed. It was not how I'd pictured the moment. I felt as though I'd been caught enacting a dirty fantasy.

And actually, I had been: You see, O. isn't my boyfriend anymore…he's my fiancé. We're getting married in August. The cake plate, the cake pans—all wedding gifts. And the role I was so eagerly trying on that night? Gracious hostess, princess bride, devoted wife. Nothing I've ever done has given me more of a thrill or caused me more shame.

I don't know which is worse: the baking or the wedding. Growing up under the tutelage of women who had only recently had their consciousness raised by Betty Friedan et. al., I was constantly reminded to avoid the sinkhole of domesticity. "Never learn to cook, girls," one of my friends' mothers used to warn us. "Because if you do, that's all you'll do for the rest of your life." Still, that doesn't fully explain my discomfort. With college, graduate school, and 10 years of a publishing career under my belt, I'm unlikely to find my options reduced to a skillet and a spatula anytime soon.

And while "Consumerism before feminism" could easily be the motto of the exploding domestic porn market and the wedding industry (or as O. calls it, the Marital Industrial Complex), that's a battle I've been fighting (and losing) with myself for years. Barneys would be a lot poorer and Planned Parenthood a lot richer if I always put my

ELLE   WWW.ELLE.COM

1.

**1. Monthly fashion magazine
Elle, UK
'The Guilty Bride'
Autumn Whitehurst, 2003**

Despite an intensive and time-consuming working method, Autumn Whitehurst strives to create editorial illustrations that capture a sense of place, that have an atmosphere, a sex appeal and are 'compositionally solid'. Working from her studio in New York City, she created this image for British Elle, turning the project around from brief to final artwork within a two-week deadline.

Book Publishing

Arguably, it was the book that was the first true medium for illustrators, and the relationship between written language and the illustrated image is a special one. This began with the illuminated religious manuscripts created between the 7th and 9th centuries, and continued with the birth of print in 1455. Until the invention of the camera and photography in 1839, illustration was the only form that printed images could take. Since photographic representation became the norm, the popularity of the illustrated image has been in decline. Within publishing now, the sectors most responsive to the work of illustrators are those of children's books, fiction titles and sometimes technical reference books, although increasingly these have turned towards using photography.

Children's Books

There is, for many illustrators, something quite unique about creating illustrations for books. It may be the special affinity that illustrators feel for the book as an object; many were first introduced to illustration through books as a child, many collect illustrated books and most illustrators use books on a regular basis for referencing images and locating facts

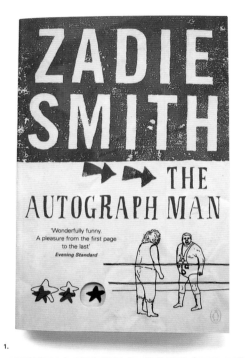

1.

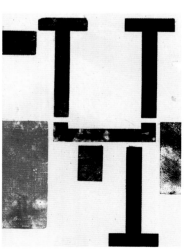

3.

4.

1 & 2. Jacket design for adult fiction
'The Autograph Man' by Zadie Smith
(Penguin, 2003)
Roderick Mills, 2003

3 & 4. Type and textural treatments
'The Autograph Man' by Zadie Smith
(Penguin, 2003)
Roderick Mills, 2003

Publishers will often commission specific jacket designs for hardback editions of fiction titles that may differ, wholly or partially, from the final jacket design used on the paperback version. In some instances the typographic treatment of the design and the illustration are fully integrated, as in this example.

and information. Nowadays illustrators are generally commissioned to either create entire children's books, often writing as well as illustrating the stories, or to produce front cover or jacket illustrations. Both areas can offer extremely rewarding commissions, artistically if not financially, as often there is a reasonable amount of time in which to produce the work. If working on a cover for a fiction title there is often enough time to read the manuscript fully and produce first stage visuals before embarking upon the final artwork.

The visuals expected for illustrated book titles differ from newspaper and magazine commissions; artists are required to create very finished early versions of what will become the final artwork. The visuals will detail the position of every element within an image and will also include very detailed finished drawings of each of the book's central characters.

For the writer/illustrator working on both text and image for a children's title, there is a much longer lead-in time. The first stage of the process, following the initial briefing, leads to the creation of a number of dummy spreads that are presented at trade book fairs to gauge the appeal and the reaction to the concept, style and approach of the book. Feedback given now can be just the first of many stages in a long line that may influence the direction that the book begins to take.

Artistic and Editorial Control

A book requires far more financial investment from a publishing company than any output from an editorial publisher. In order to recoup the initial expenses and move into creating a profit, books are expected to sell for a far longer period of time than the day or the month that a newspaper or magazine is on the shelf for. Ensuring that the product suits the intended audience, continues to sell after the publication date and remains relevant and fresh are all aspects that publishers take very seriously. With greater financial and commercial risk, it is understandable that greater artistic and editorial control rests with the publisher.

Art direction during the development of a book can come from many quarters. The art director or designer will view every illustration during a project and so too will the book's editor and editorial team, as essentially the initial commission can have come from either department. Equally important, within the process, are the

5.

6.

7.

thoughts and comments of the marketing department, since marketing plays a huge role in determining the success of a book. Books can sell or be left on the shelf depending on public reaction to the cover, and increasingly little is left to chance in this area. Feedback will reflect the saleability of the book's design. Requests from marketing and sales departments may include changes to colours, increases in type sizes and the inclusion of particular images.

One further aspect of what may seem an elongated process of commission can come into play even after every other department has approved both illustration and the design of a book. Well-known authors can demand approval rights for any jacket designs for their works and, despite being a rare occurrence, can send any jacket back to the drawing board.

Understanding the context of the book both artistically and commercially, the visual translation of the text as well as the overall creation of a design that appeals to an audience, are both fundamental aspects of successful book illustration.

5–7. Jacket and page design for adult fiction
Us & Them by Paul Davis (Laurence King, 2004)
Paul Davis, 2004

Illustrators with a proven track record and a strong concept for a book project may find that their proposals reach full production. A simple idea of how UK and US citizens view each other culminated in this book, written and illustrated by UK illustrator and commentator Paul Davis. This title is proof that even in a relatively conservative sector of the industry, strong concepts married to a strong visual style can break new ground in hitting the high-street bookshops.

**1–3. Children's Book
'The Panther Sale'
The Panther Sale (Lirabelle)
Rosie Scott, 2003**

Design and illustration approaches vary enormously within children's book publishing. Some of the best work created combines techniques that encompass simple bold drawing and a system of reduction – ensuring that simplicity communicates the narrative.

1.

2.

3.

The Book Illustrator

An Interview with Sara Fanelli

Illustrations created for books play a huge role in bringing a text to life. How do you start the process of creating your images, and when you also create the text, which comes first?

SF – After reading the text, I ask myself what aspect or issue I wish to explore with the visual comment and try to portray that. When I work on children's stories often the idea starts from a visual image. As Quentin Blake said before, this is one great thing about being the author as well as the illustrator: you can write a story about things you like drawing.

Which illustrated children's books were important to you as a child and why?

SF – I loved the atmosphere of a book. I was mainly attracted to the world that was depicted and contained within, and how I could enter it. I feel very privileged now to have the chance to create such worlds for the imagination. I also enjoyed the colours and was fascinated by details, for example in looking for the reoccurring detail of the worm (in Italian 'Zigozago') in Richard Scarry's books. I also had a book with photographic

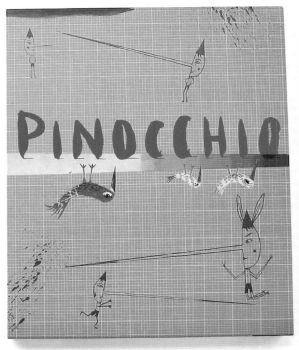

4.

4–6. Jacket and page design for children's fiction 'Pinocchio' by Sara Fanelli (Walker Books, 2003)
Sara Fanelli, 2003

A genuine twist on a children's classic gave Sara Fanelli plenty of scope to create a brand new aesthetic for this popular story. Combining her own typographic treatment with collaged elements and drawings gives the work a modern feel without losing the ageless quality of the tale itself.

5.

6.

"If the text is good it's better to offer a picture that shows a less obvious detail, or that gives an unexpected visual slant to the text."

illustrations and its unusual look was intriguing and special.

The illustrated book in its simplest form is a sequential set of images that correspond to a narrative – how do you decide which parts of the story need illustrating?

SF – I am not very interested in depicting exactly the same things that are described in the text. If the text is good it's better to let the words describe and suggest the image directly to the reader's imagination, and to offer instead a picture that shows a less obvious detail, or that gives an unexpected visual slant to the text.

The development of ideas and visuals is part of the working process for an illustrator; how many stages does your own work take and at what point do you show the publishers the work?

It is important for me to have a clear idea of the book before speaking to a publisher. I am open to and welcome sensitive editorial input and I am aware that things will change after my initial presentation, but it is good to start with some certainties.

Some books take longer at the initial stage, but then progress smoothly and others, which at first seem smooth might eventually take longer. It is a very organic process and it is important to have the ability to be open to the comments from editors whilst remaining clear about what the original vision and inspiration for the book was.

Please give a brief outline of your intentions when making illustrations for this sector of the industry?

SF – I try to make a book as I like it and would have liked it as a child. I think books come out better this way than if one tries to guess what children would generally like in their books. There is enough of a child in ourselves to know what we liked when we were younger (and still like!), and enough of an adult in a child for them to know when someone is patronising them.

Fashion Illustration

For some the term illustration is synonymous with the work of fashion illustrators, despite it losing much ground to photography since its height of popularity in the 1930s. Fashion illustration has moved gradually away from documenting the work of fashion designers for magazines, although sketched images have remained the starting point for many fashion designers as they visualise on paper the structure and fabrics for the garments that they are designing.

For the illustrator not trained as a fashion designer who wants to work in this field, it is wise to undertake the discipline with a clear understanding of who to approach for commissions, as opportunities may be less visibly flagged than other areas of the discipline.

Opportunities

Occasionally art directors cut against the tide of photographic imagery to offer illustrators the opportunity to create fresher, more personal interpretations of the season's trends and ranges. This type of fashion story commission usually comes from the fashion monthlies. It's mainly the more upmarket magazines as well as men's titles that tend to opt for this approach. The more avant-garde and independent the title, the more they are expected to be directional in their approach; in fact it is this type of fashion illustration that is considered to lead the entire discipline stylistically.

Outside of the fashion and 'style' press, the recent rise in the recognition of fashion illustration can be attributed to a number of independent clothing labels, as well as bigger brands with an understanding of marketing to youth audiences.

1.

Cult clothing labels such as A Bathing Ape in Japan, Silas in the UK and Huntergatherer in the US all began to use illustration in original and fresh ways that led some larger corporate companies to follow suit. Nike, Adidas, Levi's and Diesel have all developed ranges of clothing with print graphics inspired or created by contemporary illustrators, or they've led marketing and advertising campaigns using the work of contemporary illustrators.

In a route similar to that of successful fashion photographers, many illustrators have started by creating low-fee, directional images for magazines, viewing them as a testing ground for their work. The transition to creating advertising and publicity for fashion labels with greater budgets and fees proves that their work has appeal and longevity. Longevity in fashion, however, may not last much longer than a couple of seasons.

Illustration and Textile Designs

Freelance textile designers endure a particularly subservient role in the fashion industry. Designs are often sold for very small fees with no retention of copyright. For the illustrator that moves into producing textile designs the payment and ownership terms can come as a genuine surprise. It is, perhaps, the enjoyment of working for another type of client in another medium that inspires most to work in this area, rather than any commercial gain. For those illustrators whose work is successful and has a high recognition factor, an invitation to create textile designs may help to ensure better rates and even the retention of copyright ownership.

Successful illustrators working across a range of textile applications have recently witnessed great interest in their work, some being commissioned to produce entire collections for fashion companies and labels. As illustration in this sector gathers greater recognition, so the scope of projects increases. With public interest in property, architecture and interiors escalating in recent years, it has come as no surprise that some fashion companies have turned their attention to a bigger canvas than the body. Many have seamlessly launched their own home interiors ranges and illustrators have capitalised by creating textile designs for duvet covers, curtains, wallpapers and towels. As fashion design has moved across the divide from clothing and into the home, so too has the flexibility and creativity of today's fashion illustrators.

2.

1 & 3. Fashion and fabric design
Scribble polo shirt
by Heartland Summer
Jeremyville, 2003

2. Bag design
Sports bag by Jeremyville, 2004
Jeremyville, 2004

Sydney-based architect turned graphic designer and illustrator Jeremy sells this printed polo shirt on-line and through his own store in Paddington, Sydney. The work highlights his overwhelming interest in the drawn and doodled image.

Objects such as bags give a rare opportunity to create work for a different kind of canvas. These items will often be fashion-related and may only be available for one season, still a lot longer than the lifespan of a daily newspaper or an average magazine.

1.

2.

**1 & 2. Fabric design
Psychedelic Poolside Dream
swimwear by JG4B
Jasper Goodall, 2005**

For his second range of limited
edition bikinis, British illustrator Jasper
Goodall created fabric designs inspired by
psychedelic and tropical colours, as well
as serpents and sea creatures. Known for
his work as a fashion illustrator, it was
not an unexpected move for Goodall to
make, in creating his own fashion range.

The Fashion Illustrator

An Interview with Stina Persson

Illustration and fashion are inextricably linked and in
recent years the relationship between the two has
blossomed further. Why do you think this has happened
and how does your work fit into this relationship?

SP – I think the balance between the use of photography
and illustration in the fashion world was off for quite
some time. Art directors and editors at magazines
seemed to be scared of illustration and the element of
unexpectedness that it brings. But now that everything is
digital and can be controlled and manipulated, maybe the
longing for the uncontrolled has come back.

My work is quite clearly non-photographic and lacks a
certain Adobe Illustrator look that was popular in fashion
illustration for a while. I think this human, rough, and
original touch can be appealing.

The figure plays a prominent role in much of your work,
how crucial is drawing from life, even outside of your
commissioned work?

3.

SP – Drawing from life is necessary to train your eye. And that's what it's all about; a good eye. On the other hand it's both a luxury and time consuming. Therefore I, as I think most illustrators do today, work from flat reference material, such as magazine clippings, photographs or even digital snapshots of posing family and friends. After all, there are deadlines to meet.

Fashion can be a notoriously fickle industry and with your work appearing in numerous major publications and companies, how do you ensure that it remains fresh and forward-looking?

SP – To keep work fresh is one of my biggest struggles as I think that this either makes or breaks the final piece. And it's not always easy in a commercial world when ten people have different ideas of how a hand should be held or what percentage of magenta a watercolour shade should be in. But that's also the challenge of creating work commercially.

My way to deal with this has been to do several drawings until one feels fresh and quick. It should look effortless. Which takes... effort. If it doesn't happen on one piece of paper I assemble the final piece digitally from several drawings.

More generally, consciously keeping my style modern and up-to-date is not my main aim – there are so many other illustrators who are amazing at it. I just try to do what I'm doing and not get stuck in a routine. If it looks modern to people, that's good.

Do you approach illustration projects with any predetermined notions of how the finished piece will work and how many attempts do you create before you are happy with the results?

SP – I wish I didn't have to have a finished image in my head as I work – so that you could always be open to what the piece needs and ready to make something cool out of a mistake. But commercially that wouldn't work as you have to submit first a rough sketch and later a finished sketch. I've almost succeeded in convincing my clients that the rough really is just rough for me, as the finished image is done in watercolour and needs to be at least a little unpredictable.

Please give a brief outline of your intentions when making illustrations for this sector of the industry?

SP – I've somehow found myself in a special niche of fashion illustration that I think sometimes is forgotten. Since fashion illustration became 'in vogue' again a lot of companies and publications not dealing in fashion directly have started to want some of that fashion look to rub off on them. This is what I've done to a large extent; a lot of fashionable-looking work, only a small part of which is directly related to the fashion industry. Instead, I've worked for everyone from Volvo to French aperitifs... Maybe this extended use of fashion illustration also adds to the feeling that fashion illustration is everywhere.

4.

3 & 4. Various fabric designs by Bjorn Borg Stina Persson, 2003

Fashion-inspired, funky and abstract designs created for tennis icon Bjorn Borg's fashion label. The images work as illustrations on the fabric rather than as all-over designs – fulfilling that demand to be 'read' rather than just forming part of the overall look.

"I do several drawings until one feels fresh and quick. It should look effortless. Which takes... effort."

Advertising Illustration

Advertising is a tough sector to break into and is not for the faint-hearted; it can be a brutal environment for the freelance illustrator. In return for punishing schedules, unrealistic deadlines, lack of creative decision-making and being told what to do and sometimes how to do it, there is, however, the promise of the advertising fee. It is generally recognised that an increase in fees equates to the increased pressure felt when undertaking most advertising commissions.

Agency Structures

All advertising agencies are structurally similar. Within the art department an art director will work hand-in-hand with a copywriter under the head of art or the creative director, normally responsible for a number of similar two-person creative teams/partnerships. Art directors create the visual properties whilst the copywriter creates the written word or spoken script, for any advertising campaign.

Working alongside the art department of an advertising agency is the art-buying department. This manages the freelance sources of artwork: the photographers, model-makers, directors, animators and illustrators. The art buyer keeps abreast of developments, trends, fashions and movements in each of the key disciplines by attending exhibition openings, scouring the art and design press and constantly calling in portfolios of work from individual practitioners and agencies representing the best in contemporary work. The art-buying department handles a vital aspect of the day-to-day running of an advertising agency, as much of the talent utilised in

Despite the frustrations of working in advertising, the opportunity for visual creativity outside of the norm is of genuine appeal to most illustrators.

the creation and production of any advertising campaign is bought in, hired especially for the project.

The account handler ensures the relationship between the advertising agency and the client runs smoothly, their main role is to liaise and coordinate each project for the agency and client. They are also responsible for making presentations of creative work to the client, sometimes without a member of the creative team and certainly always without the illustrator present. Sitting outside of the creative loop can lead to frustration for the freelance illustrator; client responses, changes and alterations to visuals or artwork are all relayed via the account handler. Be warned, this is a line of communication longer than the illustrator may find beneficial.

Coverage

A strong advertising campaign will aim to immerse itself and the product into the public's subconscious. It will seek to present an idea and an image for that product that becomes instantly recognisable, creating brand awareness and a product personality. Advertising utilises a range of media in its pursuit of brand/product recognition: from posters on billboards, bus sides and shelters, referred to as 'outdoor media', to TV and cinema commercials known as 'on-air media'. The scope is endless and to the illustrator working on an advertising campaign, the effect of such coverage can be enormous.

In recent years campaigns have become less regional and more international. With increased outlets for advertising, there is greater public recognition of campaigns and the associated product. Running hand-in-hand with this are the associations made with the illustration style and the visual identity of the campaign. This can be hugely beneficial if the product is deemed 'cool' or has entered the public zeitgeist as it encourages other companies to commission the same illustrator, hoping for associations to be made. More frequent though, is the downside; the work remains connected to a product long after any

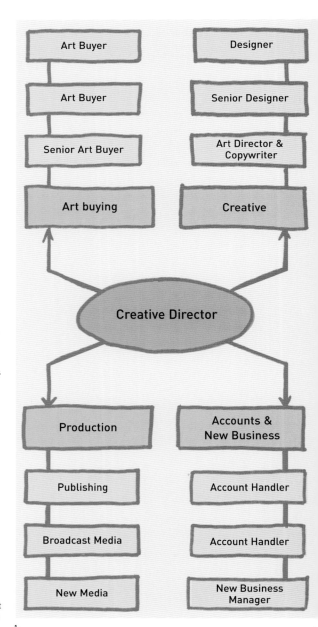

1.

2–4. Press, Web and TV advertising 'Think About It' by Kia Motors Pete Fowler for Mustoes Design Agency, 2004

An advertising campaign for Kia Motors saw Pete Fowler create a range of applications that were used in various media across the campaign. Unique type design, character design as well as animated sequences for use on TV and in Web-based promotions gave the company a branding that stood apart from mainstream car manufacturers' advertising offerings.

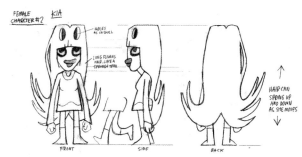

2.

1. Advertising agency structures

The complexity of agency structures is compounded by the terminology. It pays to understand where your contact stands within the department hierarchies.

3.

4.

advertising campaign has ceased to run. This stylistic link can prove detrimental in bringing in new advertising commissions, the visual associations with previous products being too strong to risk attempting to create new visual links. The reality can mean that even the hardest working illustrators are only likely to be commissioned for very visible campaigns every other year at the most.

Media Appeal

Despite the frustrations of working in advertising, the opportunity for visual creativity outside of the norm is of genuine appeal to most illustrators. Seeing your work emblazoned across a billboard, plastered on the side of a taxi, or moving across the commercial breaks on TV is a very exciting incentive. Whilst working in this sector of the business remains elusive to many, the appeal can't be underestimated. For those illustrators who rarely step outside of editorial commissions, working constantly on a canvas no larger than a single sheet of paper, the opportunity of creating an image that has to work visually on a 52-sheet billboard poster is an undeniable challenge.

Steep Learning Curves

Advertising offers many of these unique challenges; most too must be resolved within an incredibly short time-span. An advertising art director may view a portfolio of illustration work but see the potential, for example, in using the artist for a TV commercial. This may be despite the illustrator having little or no direct previous involvement in animation.

➡

He may be called upon to work on ideas, themes and storyboards for an animated commercial and if the initial stage is successful, the illustrator may then be required to embark on a collaboration throughout the project with an animation house. It is quite possible that advertising space has been booked and the deadline for the artistic creation, the final production and the delivery to the client has been set before the illustrator has even been informed of the project. Most illustrators enjoy rising to this type of challenge in the pursuit of creative work.

Art Buying

Art buyers have a tendency to call in a range of portfolios from numerous solo illustrators and agents for a creative team to review before making any final decisions about the choice of artist for the commission. It is also known for clients to be shown the work of illustrators by account handlers prior to the illustrator being informed that the job is potentially theirs. This can create a useful platform for fee negotiation if the job does come to fruition, but it can also cause havoc for the illustrator who likes to keep abreast of the flow of work at any one time. Inevitably, once the commission has started, advertising art directors expect the illustrator to be immediately available throughout the life of the project and conveniently tend to forget that the artist will have regular clients, even if they are offering a much lower fee.

Illustrators and their agents can find that they are constantly organising the delivery of portfolios to advertising agents for projects that rarely lead on to real work. Advertising is one sector of the market that has been slow to adopt new ways of viewing work, preferring to view real-time leather-bound portfolios rather than digital versions on-line. This reluctance to move forward may be related to the fact that art buyers wish to retain some mystery and status in their positions and see the on-line viewing of portfolios as a threat to their existence. Whatever the reason, courier companies are not unhappy with this arrangement; at any one time they are responsible for moving numerous portfolios of work from illustrators, and other freelance creatives, to agencies and back again.

Advertising Fees

Once a portfolio of work has been reviewed and the illustrator seen as potentially the right candidate for the project, a period of negotiation will commence. Advertising fees work in a way that differs from any other sector of illustration. Very rarely

1.

2.

1. **Press campaign**
2. **Animation storyboard**
3. **TV commercial stills**
'Think About It' by Kia Motors
Peter Fowler for Mustoes Design
Agency, 2004
Creative team
Mick Mahoney & Andy Amadeo
Production Company
Passion Pictures
Director
Pete Candeland

A project of this complexity takes time as well as extremely coordinated organisation. Normally an agency will develop a pitch for an advertising campaign following the project briefing and once it has client approval the illustrator is drafted into the project.

does the agency reveal the fee that they wish to pay for the work at the outset. A normal discussion about the payment for the job will start with the agency detailing the client, the product, the number of images required, the media that the work is expected to run across, the period of time that the work will be used for and the deadline for delivery. Any one or combination of these factors can affect the outcome of the discussions.

Quoting for Work

Creating a quotation for a job will often require meticulous planning with attention to the smallest detail. It can be a time-consuming task – one good reason why many illustrators work through an agent – and the lengthy task of creating a quote will not always result in the job being commissioned. Many account handlers require rough figures to discuss with the end client and will take a range of quotes and portfolios into meetings to help decide on the right person for the job. Spending time working on a fee breakdown for a job that may well not occur can be frustrating and disheartening, especially for those who spend more time creating quotes for illustrations.

Test Images

With budgets and fees getting tighter as advertising agencies – the first to suffer in times of recession – demand value for money, the element of chance in a commission has been removed by some agencies. Rather than take expensive risks at visuals and artwork stage, a new system of commencing a project has emerged. Increasingly, not only does the illustrator have to win the job on merit – often against stiff competition, and provide a quotation, often for a complex set of criteria – he or she can now be asked to provide a test image. A test should not be confused with a first stage visual; it is an opportunity for the agency to request an image, with no usage attached, to gauge how the illustrator might tackle the job if given it. The fee for a test image is invariably low despite sometimes taking as long to create as a final illustration. The client basically wants to see the final illustration, or as close to it as possible, but for a small proportion of the final fee.

Focus Groups

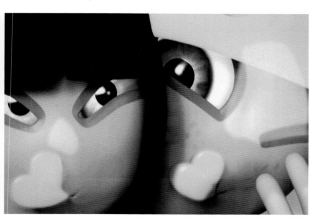

Even after submission of the test, it can still take an agency and client some time to come to a final decision. Many clients unwilling to trust their instincts, decide to test the work using a Focus Group where the general public is used for market research. Illustration fares particularly badly in these tests, as the general public is generally unaware of how the discipline works or how to rationalise its response to it.

Pitching

Similar to the test image is the pitch, both the paid and unpaid. Pitching exists across the design and advertising industries, despite leading organisations that support good practice advising against unpaid involvement. Many commercial artists claim that this is almost impossible not to do, as more and more clients, seeking to gain valuable input into a project, trawl the desperate creative industries. In truth, there are more design companies than the industry can support, a fact that is recognised and exploited.

Most pitching for work is undertaken by advertising agencies and design companies, but the knock-on effect ensures that illustrators are being commissioned to create images for these pitches. Low fees without any guarantee of a real project, equate to a risk being carried by the illustrator as well as the design or advertising group.

Illustrating for advertising agencies and their clients is not without difficulties, but most will explain that the pros far out-weigh the cons. The potential for working across a range of new media, for higher fees than in other sectors, on high profile projects, retains, despite all the difficulties, great appeal.

3.

1.

The Advertising Illustrator

An Interview with Henry Obasi

Working as an illustrator on advertising commissions puts your work in front of a massive audience; do you find this a creative challenge or is it like any other project?

HO – This can be regarded as a challenge but not a major one. No matter how large the audience, advertising companies usually commission specific illustrators to engage with a target-specific audience. This is mainly because they are aware of the audience's social cultural characteristic and how that audience will respond to the artist's visual style. Most of the pressure to define the audience has been taken off by this stage of commissioning.

When I was commissioned to do the Playstation 2 press campaign I was brought in because my illustrative style was considered appropriate for the project. I was told in the brief who the target audience was and what was required of me stylistically for the campaign. The large audience became a ready-made recipient to viewing my work en masse. The only challenge from then on is to produce good work as standard!

Advertising is seen as the most financially rewarding sector for an illustrator to work in; what are the other benefits you can relate to?

HO – Advertising campaigns provide a clearly-defined audience to view your work on a larger platform (usually internationally or at the very least nationally). Having your work seen by both a global and national audience in one hit is one of the most gratifying accolades. Working with a large brand gives the chance of my illustration being seen worldwide, and this elevates my status as an illustrator as you become recognisable beyond the small arenas of popular culture. This also brings me to the attention of possible overseas clients. It is very hard to divorce the financial rewards of doing a large advertising campaign from anything else because all the benefits feed each other.

You've produced work for a range of advertising clients – does it mean that your work becomes synonymous with the brands that you've helped to advertise?

HO – If you have worked primarily with one brand in particular, it is common sense that the audience will naturally associate the illustrator with that brand. But more importantly other brands will associate you with that brand. This can be both a blessing and a curse, especially with fashion brands, where competition is fierce.

I did a high profile campaign for a fashion label a few years ago. The exposure was good and the campaign lasted a while, but this had the detrimental effect of aligning my illustration style with that label. It became increasingly obvious that it would be a while before I would be able to work with another big fashion brand, especially as my style of illustration is considered niche. However, the plus side was that other big brands from different market sectors noticed my work and subsequently commissioned me. Working on a major ad campaign had given me validation in their eyes.

2.

Working with a large brand gives the chance of my illustration being seen worldwide. This elevates my status as an illustrator, you become recognisable beyond the small arenas of popular culture."

Get live commentary, up to the minute scores, match reports and video clips of the goals on Orange World.
Visit Orange World on your phone or www.orange.co.uk/bolton for more information.
Official Communications Partner of Bolton Wanderers FC.

orange™

Advertising deadlines are often very short. Do you adjust your working methods to suit this and how many stages does your work go through for advertising clients?

HO – Workflow now has had to change from the old days. It is no longer possible to spend three months painting the figurehead of a bank for a corporate brochure. The working process for creating images is of paramount importance in an arena where reception to visual stimuli is instantaneous and then forgotten. This digital age has forced the viewer, be it the art director, client or target audience, to expect visual data almost immediately. This ideal carries through in all parts of our lives. Whether we are waiting for emails to download, purchasing music from Apple's iTunes music store, or having the pizza man deliver a Stuffed Crust. We want everything now and this is apparent when delivering artwork to the client.

Most illustrators have now adapted their style to fit a more speedy workflow. Initially I created all my illustrations using a mixture of drawing and screenprinting, but I soon found that this was not time-effective (or, more seriously, cost-effective). When you have clients requesting amendments every five minutes you have to up your game! that time there were almost five different stages to my working process and each stage was nearly a day long. Now I have got it down to 2–3 stages that last a fraction of the time. I can complete a commission from rough to finish in anything from a couple of hours to a couple of days.

Please give a brief outline of your intentions when making illustrations for this sector of the industry?

HO – I need to try and communicate some of my own messages through my work, whether stylistically through mark-making or through art directive interplay. By this I mean being involved in the communicative process of a campaign. Usually art directors commission illustrators to re-dress their rather fixed ideas. This position of no-involvement relegates the illustrator to no more than decorator. At times this is cool – sometimes the advertising message being communicated is ultra specific. The fear of any external factors being brought into the mix by the illustrator can be perceived as possibly being detrimental, especially when big bucks are involved. But when the illustrator is given a chance to inject artistic quality other than their drawing style, it is a bonus.

When working with Mother on a campaign for Orange, I was able to express humour in my work. By being involved from the initial stages I could introduce creative elements. As with most artists, all illustrators want to be recognised at some level and that is no different for me. I want people to see my work and enjoy it at the very least. If the campaign works and gets people to spend their money, then that is a bonus!

**1–3. Press advertising
'Goal' by Orange
Henry Obasi for Mother, 2003**

Illustration is the perfect medium for this press campaign for Orange's sports update service on Orange World. This way they've had no problems with sponsorship or the rights to use images of particular sports, stars or teams. These images by Henry Obasi give the service a new dimension.

Music Industry Illustration

For many, illustration is seen as the discipline that visualises text, but another key aspect lies in its ability to give music a visual form. For each illustrator introduced to the discipline at an early age through children's books, there is another that has found illustration as a teenager, predominantly through an interest in popular music.

Music graphics have played a definitive role in shaping the way that we relate to the music that we hear, creating an identity and personality for the product in a visual form. Long gone are the days when record companies could simply create an album sleeve by using a photograph of the artist alone on the cover. Far more unique and sophisticated solutions aid sales through sleeve design that projects a graphic image of the artist.

Record Label Set-Ups

The music business is a global industry that employs tens of thousands of people and represents artists and acts that generate many millions of dollars per annum. The huge scale of the operation means that finding in-roads into working as a freelance illustrator can be less than straightforward. Large record labels normally run their own art departments, creating sleeves and promos for their acts on an in-house basis, buying in photography and illustration on a project-by-project basis. Some of the large labels, however, prefer to out-source all of their design, working with one major design company or a selection of smaller agencies, commissioning them for the entire design and production of each project.

Gaining access to information and contact details for both record label art departments and independent design companies, although not initially as simple as in other sectors of the design and advertising industries, will prove fruitful. A little more 'homework', coupled with an awareness of current and emerging trends in both music and design practice within the discipline, is necessary. Frequent visits to record stores and regular checking of the small-print credits in the sleeve notes will elicit the correct contact information, or at least work as a starting point. Increasingly individual acts now have their own website where further contact information can be obtained. Undertaking research is the best preparation for reaching contacts, particularly in this field.

It is rare for an illustrator to work for a particular band throughout their entire lifespan, but it can happen. The spin-offs can be as interesting and challenging as facets of advertising illustration. Creating images for merchandise, back-drops and set design, as well as animations for the band's promo videos are all areas that can open up for those whose work defines the graphic look of a recording artist. For some musicians, the very nature of working with an illustrator is seen fondly as rekindling their own art school beginnings, the art school having acted as a breeding ground for bands since the 1960s.

1.

1–5. Music promotion 'Mish mash' club poster for Cargo nightclub Insect, 2004

Insect was commissioned to create a series of promotional posters for Mish Mash, an independent club night at Cargo in Hoxton, London. Many independent record labels and clubs require promotional material and this can be an interesting, if not lucrative, field to gain valuable experience in.

2.

3.

4.

5.

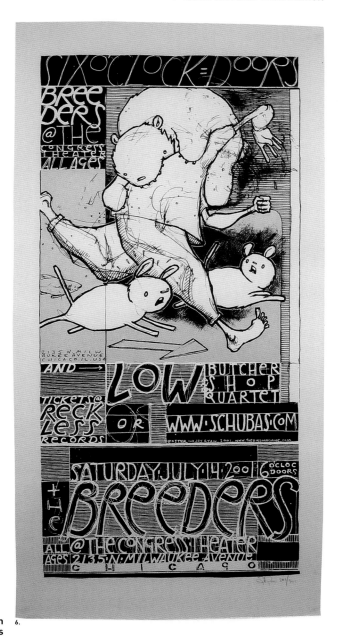

6.

**6. Music Promotion
Gig poster for the Breeders
for Congress Theatre, Chicago.
Jay Ryan, 2001**

Jay Ryan of The Bird Machine, based in
Chicago, creates editioned silk-screen
prints as promotional posters for gigs at
various venues. Employing images that
communicate immediately and directly,
Ryan works with a limited colour palette
that translates to the medium perfectly.

1.

1. Music Promotion
Gig poster for Interpol
for Rock City, Nottingham
Jay Ryan, 2004

The Music Industry Illustrator

An Interview with Kustaa Saksi

Working for the music industry brings another dimension to the job of the illustrator who is normally associated with bringing text to life. In this sector it is about bringing a visual form to music and it can also be associated with fashions and trends. How do you respond to a given project?

KS – Well, it really depends on the project. Sometimes the client is open and sometimes they come with a clearly thought-out idea. Both are fine with me. Of course I prefer illustrating the music I like, but sometimes it can be really refreshing to do something completely different.

Record sleeve design has been a vital aspect of marketing music; when CDs emerged to replace vinyl, the canvas reduced dramatically. Do you enjoy the restrictions of the medium?

KS – I still prefer vinyl format and fortunately I've been working with record companies who usually publish in vinyl too. Nowadays, the clumsy 1970s CD jewel case may be a classic, but I usually prefer the cardboard ones. It really is a challenge to make the small CD format appealing. But I wonder what we are going to do with MP3s?

The perception by the audience of a musician or recording artist is often drawn from the graphics created for their recordings – do you have the artist's visual identity in mind whilst you create their cover art?

KS – Sure. But I prefer covers that take the listener to a different level. I think the covers can be a bit challenging too – I always try to illustrate the moods and feelings from the music. Of course it's just my personal view, but I hope it opens the music up to other people too.

Your work has a surreal, other-worldly feel about it – do you think that it has helped you get work in this area of design?

KS – Well, it's really difficult to say. Sometimes the music makes me draw different things. It's really about the music and how it matches with the illustration. Hopefully one day I can do a project where the image is first.

Please give a brief outline of your intentions when making illustrations for this sector of the industry?

KS – Well, first, hopefully I like the music I'm going to illustrate. If I do, I usually get stuck into it for some time. And then I get deeper and try to understand it. After that it's easy and inspiring to make my work. But if I don't like the stuff – then it's like any other work project, good or bad, but I don't take it too personally.

2.

2 & 3. CD cover design
'Country Falls' by Husky Rescue
Catskills Records, 2003
Kustaa Saksi, 2003

Surreal landscapes and imagery represent
the 'Country Falls' album artwork for
Husky Rescue. Finnish illustrator Saksi
divides his time creating work for clients
in the music industry and in magazine
publishing and advertising.

3.

"I always try to illustrate the
moods and feelings from
the music. Of course it's
just my personal view, but
I hope it opens the music
up to other people too."

Graphic Design Studio Collaboration

Whilst many aspects of the communication design industry are contained within specialised compartments and departments, as we have seen with advertising, magazine, newspaper and book publishing, there are a vast number of design companies that exist to offer broader services.

Independent graphic design studios and companies far outnumber the specialist advertising agencies or publishing companies, and are a rich source of work for the illustrator. Commissions can be forthcoming for any type of project; illustrators are called in to create images for annual reports, to work on logo designs, produce cover illustrations for financial reports, artwork for theatre posters – the list is endless. As in other aspects of the industry, knowing the specialist nature of each company is vital before approaching them with requests for meetings or portfolio reviews. Following the international design press and researching company websites is the best way of gleaning up-to-date information about projects undertaken by these independent companies.

Working Relationships

The working relationship for both illustrator and the design company is an important one and much of the success in any collaboration relies on a level of trust between both parties. For the designer commissioning the illustrator, he or she must feel confident that the work is delivered within the deadline and is of a standard that matches previous work in the artist's portfolio. The illustrator must trust that the designer will use his work

in a respectful and professional way; not running type over an image or cropping, or cutting off the sides of the artwork without prior consultation.

Working relationships can take time to build, but the key to ensuring a project runs successfully and smoothly lies in open lines of communication; regular conversations on the phone or via email to update the designer on how the illustration is taking shape can be very useful.

It is wise, when working for a new client, to build into the schedule an extra stage to show the artwork in progress. This stage sits between the viewing of the visuals and the artwork and can be used to ensure that all elements within the image are present and correct. Some illustrators produce a black-and-white line version of their intended artwork to help the designer visualise how the final illustration will look.

Contracts and Purchase Orders

To ensure that both parties fully understand the process of the commission, it can be useful for a contract or purchase order to be issued by the design company to the illustrator. Incorporated into the contract must be a description of the job itself, the fee, and specified deadline for submission of the work, as well as payment terms and conditions.

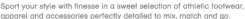

Sport your style with finesse in a sweet selection of athletic footwear, apparel and accessories perfectly detailed to mix, match and go.

For the Finish Line nearest you call toll-free 1-877-777-FINL

1.

Independent graphic design studios and companies far out-number the specialist advertising agencies or publishing companies and are a rich source of work for the illustrator.

Unfortunately not every company adheres to the principle of the contract or purchase order and practice across the industry varies. It is rare, for example, for a magazine in the UK to issue a purchase order, but standard practice for a similar company in the US. The purchase order, or PO, exists to protect both the client and illustrator, a signed PO ensures that the artist can invoice for the fee agreed at the start of the job and that is documented on the paperwork. This method avoids the need to rely on word-of-mouth or vague recollection of the details of any discussion, and is useful for commissions that may run into weeks or even months. Good practice means that an accounts department will not have to seek authorisation to make a payment after the invoice has arrived if a contract or PO number is quoted on the invoice. See examples of these on p.168–171. The contract and the PO are really ways of standardising written agreements. If the company does not have templates for these available, ask for the agreement in writing as a formality.

1. Promotional campaign
Maddie – Nike Finish-line
Nike 2005
Vault 49 with Cinco Design, 2005

Vault 49, based in New York, collaborated with Cinco Design, in Portland Oregon, home to the global headquarters of Nike, to create a promotional campaign for the sportswear manufacturers. Combining photography and drawn hand-rendered illustration, the images define an aspirational and fresh look for Maddie, a range of female attire.

1.

**1. Character development
Alpha and Bravo – Skyflyers
British Airways
Tado for Fitch International, 2004**

Tado working with Fitch International, re-branded the British Airways' 'Sky-Flyers' children's club. Tado, Mike Doney and Katie Tang, created the two characters Alpha and Bravo, which Fitch International then utilised extensively throughout branding, merchandise and marketing in print and on-line. Life-sized mascots of the characters were also created for promotional events.

The Collaborative Illustrator

An Interview with Anthony Burrill

Working with design companies differs from working in other sectors of the market – there is more crossover and collaboration between designer and illustrator/image-maker. How do you feel that this has advantaged your work?

AB – When working for an ad agency the traditional hierarchies are well understood by everybody involved. Normally I have the most contact with the art director during the job. The agency then deals with the client; there isn't much direct communication. When working with design companies there tends to be much more contact with everybody involved. It feels like there is much more collaboration. Projects tend to develop at a slower pace with design companies. There are more stages involved and a greater lead-in time to production. I feel that clients get more out of me when I'm more involved in the project, rather than just being a stylist.

At what stage in a project do you ideally like to be involved and how many stages do you normally envisage a project taking?

AB – Ideally I'd like to be involved right at the start. In practice it tends to be quite a long way in. sometimes you are asked to pitch for a job. I don't think anybody enjoys pitching for work, I try to avoid it if possible. Sometimes people pay for pitches, which helps the motivation and it feels more 'real'. That helps you to get thinking about a project. Usually the pitch work doesn't take that long. if there is a small shortlist of possible designers it shouldn't be too hard to pick the right person for the job. After the pitch has been won it starts getting busy. Initial designs from the pitch have to be resolved and ideas have to be developed. If there are questions about style these have to be addressed too. After this initial stage there are usually another couple of rounds of revisions before final designs are presented. There are inevitable tweaks to be made on the final designs. This is usually the point where very tight deadlines get stretched a bit!

Pricing work for projects with design companies is not nearly as simple as in editorial or even advertising work – how do you find a happy medium?

AB - Most projects tend to be priced as a single design fee, rather than a daily rate. People in design always ask me what my daily rate is. I don't have one. The fee depends on the size of the project, the usage and the client. Advertising tends to be more generous, but then the pressures and deadlines are always much greater with advertising.

**2 & 3. Design studio collaboration
Mural for Bloomberg
Anthony Burrill for Scarlet
Projects, 2003**

Burrill was commissioned to create a
mural for Bloomberg, at the financial
institution's London headquarters. Vinyl
graphics were applied directly to the walls,
although the design was resolved on-
screen prior to installation.

2.

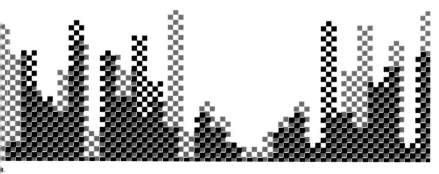

3.

*When working with design companies there
tends to be much more contact with
everybody involved. It feels like there is much
more collaboration."*

**What freedom does working with design companies
on projects allow and how does your own interpretation
of the brief lead the working process that you adopt?**

AB – I am normally approached to work on a project as
a result of people seeing my previous work – so usually
there is an understanding that they want my particular
approach. I try to think of new ways of doing things for
each project. Sometimes this doesn't work, then people
ask me to do something that I've already done before.
Every job involves compromise on both parts. The client
has a strong idea of what they want and understands the
audience they are talking to. At the end of the project I'm
always happy if I've managed to produce a piece of work
that feels like it's been the result of a good collaboration
between me and the client.

**Please give a brief outline of your intentions when
making work for this sector of the industry?**

AB – I don't really tend to approach work for design
companies in a different way to any other client. The main
thing for me is to have a good dialogue with the client.

Self-Initiated Illustration

Every illustrator enjoys the prospect of working outside of what constitutes the commission norm. For some it can be frustrating to find that after a couple of years of regular work, commissions start to become repetitive or even mundane. Keeping things alive and fresh can take the illustrator into new areas of interest and can help push one or two boundaries at the edges of the discipline.

Maintaining a progressive approach to illustration can be achieved by continuing to work independently in sketchbooks, creating new artworks and generally spending time researching and exploring new ways of visualising and new forms of expression.

Finding time to work on self-initiated projects can be problematic when an illustrator is busy with art directors and designers requesting commissions, but it is crucial in keeping one step ahead of the game. It may be as simple as taking a morning out of the studio each week to visit exhibitions and galleries, or an afternoon drawing on location. It may be a local 'life' drawing class or a print workshop, either way it can help feed the imagination, give some perspective to the activity of illustration and assist in finding new directions to work in and towards.

Linked with much self-initiated work are spin-off commercial projects. These commence because of an illustrator's desire to work in new and different areas of interest or can start purely through financial necessity when commissions are not forthcoming. Organising an independent exhibition of new work is a useful way of keeping clients informed about developments in a body of work and can be financially positive if sales are accomplished. Creating limited edition screen-prints or digital prints can mean that prices per unit can be kept reasonably low, but can accumulate as an image can be sold numerous times.

Illustrators with an eye for both fashion and business find that investing time and capital into designing and producing a small range of T-shirts can be another form of income. Small independent fashion retail outlets will often take a range of T-shirts on a sale-or-return basis and this experience can be helpful when approaching fashion companies and labels for freelance commissions.

A growth area in recent years has been in the production of 'toys'. Originally starting as promotional devices for independent record and fashion labels, a sizable interest has grown in limited-edition toy characters. Created for and aimed at an adult audience who have grown up with toy figures based on characters from movies, animations, comics and video games, the new genre concentrates on hipper, more streetwise and stylistically cool figures. Often starting life as 2D sketches within illustrators' sketchbooks or in commissioned artwork, these toys have gone from purely promotional items to collectable objects of desire.

1.

1. Self-initiated exhibition project Kiki and Milo – Mademoiselle Pretty Depressing fourxfour 222 Gallery Fafi, 2004

2. Self-initiated exhibition project Irina – Mademoiselle Pretty Depressing fourxfour 222 Gallery Fafi, 2004

For an exhibition in the Los Angeles gallery, fourxfour, French-based image-maker Fafi created a series of self-initiated pieces around the self-titled theme of Mademoiselle Pretty Depressing. Working in both 2D and 3D formats, Fafi's work investigates themes of fantasy and desire.

2.

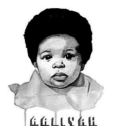

3.

3. 'Jeff', 'Aaliya', 'Kurt', 'Tupac',
'Biggie' and 'Michael' paintings from
the 'Little Angels' series
Michael Gillette, 2003

This series of portraits was originally
created as a self-initiated piece of work
for his own personal website, but was later
reproduced in print by Gillette's agent as
a promotional piece.

4. Magazine cover
New York Times magazine
'Bush'
Michael Gillette, 2004

Producing new self-initiated work in a
style that differs from that work most
recognised by clients can lead to new
commissions. British-born, San Francisco-
based Michael Gillette's portrait of George
Bush for the cover of the New York Times
is a case in point.

The Self-Initiated Illustrator

An Interview with Han Hoogerbrugge

Personal work can be the driving influence for commercial projects; how do you maintain the correct balance that best suits you?

HH – My personal work and commercial work are often close together. I get asked for commissions because of what I do with my free work and I can only do commercial jobs if they relate to my free work. Usually clients are after something kind of dark, funny and different when they commission me. This means I don't have to worry about a balance most of the time. The commercial work usually feels like the same thing as my free work.

Does your working method alter depending on the type of project, personal or commercial, that you are working on?

HH – No, I do what I do and I think that's one of the main reasons people ask me. It is definitely one of my demands when taking on a commercial job. I need to have the freedom to do things my way. Of course I listen to a client's needs and I try to give them what they want, but it should all stay within the range of the kind of thing I do.

What themes and ideas do you explore in your own work that translate to commercial projects?

HH – I try to communicate uncertain feelings with my work. Although my work is usually black and white, the ideas behind the work are grey. If I make an animation with a smoking character it shouldn't be clear if I'm against smoking or pro smoking. There should be a little of both in it. I try to leave room for the viewer to find their own personal interpretation. In the end, its meaning is decided by the viewer. Commercial work usually needs clear communication, but I always try to insert some of my greyness in it. At first the message might be clear, but on a closer look you might see something less clear.

Please give a brief outline of your intentions when making illustrations for this sector of the industry?

HH – Making money is my prime intention, if I could make enough money with my own work I probably wouldn't do commercial stuff. On the other hand it's nice to do something else every once in a while. Working on your own stuff all the time can make you blind. Commercial jobs can create a healthy distance between me and my work, and give me a better perspective on what I do – but then again, if it didn't make me money, I wouldn't do it.

"I try to communicate uncertain feelings with my work. I try to leave room for the viewer to find their own personal interpretation."

1.

1–3. Film festival promo
HAFF Leader
Holland Animation Film Festival
Han Hoogerbrugge, 2004

Han Hoogerbrugge, based in Holland, creates self-initiated and challenging, yet often controversial animations that he releases on-line through his own website. Putting himself at the centre of his work, Hoogerbrugge uses digital photographic self-portraits that he utilises as a trace-guide for his Flash-animated drawings.

2.

3.

4. MAKING IT HAPPEN

Unlike graphic design, there is not a clearly visible, tried-and-tested path into working as a freelance illustrator. Forging a career can take equal amounts of patience, skill and luck. Understanding how to market one's work, maintain client interest and build a professional reputation can be a painstaking experience.

Marketing the Product and the Art of Self-Promotion

It is quite possible that some of the very best illustration currently being created is never seeing the light of day. It will never leave the screen or the portfolio of the person creating it, as they are unable or unwilling to engage in promoting their work. Being able to market, promote and generally inform the illustration commissioners of your work is as vital to working in the field as the ability to create an image in the first place. Without a marketing campaign, even a very simple one, an illustrator can fall at the first hurdle.

As covered in the previous chapter, there are many different aspects and areas to the world of design, advertising and communication. Each offers opportunities for illustrators to win commissions and create work: the secret is in understanding how to make that first point of contact and then in maintaining the interest in your work throughout your career.

When mid-sized and large corporate companies want to extend their market share and increase sales they promote themselves. They will hire a PR company or an advertising agency, use broadcast media, create print and publishing campaigns and experiment with outdoor and indoor media. For the lone illustrator, the budget for promotion may be dramatically smaller, but the intentions are very similar.

The Right Audience

The key to positive promotion is to ensure that all communication is aimed squarely at the intended audience. Therefore, forming an up-to-date list of potential clients is as important as creating positive and worthwhile self-promotional material. The type of list can vary from illustrator to illustrator; some would class a little black book of phone numbers and contact addresses as a definitive and exhaustive resource. Others, however, would claim that a database software application that merges contact details, can be utilised to email specific groups, as well as print selected entries on to labels for mail-shot purposes is far more useful.

1.

The design, publishing and advertising worlds are different from other types of industry in that it is rare for people to stay in the same job for much more than a year or two, compared to five years elsewhere. Finding out who is working with whom and at which company can take time. Even after completing a list of art director working on magazines in New York, for instance, many will have moved jobs, gone elsewhere or moved up the food chain.

Successful illustrators who choose to represent themselves may spend an entire day a week updating mailing lists and databases, initiating meetings and sending out cards and samples, just to stay ahead of the pack. This process can be mundane and difficult to maintain when busy with work, but it is crucial to ensure a constant flow of work.

Contact Databases

It is possible to beat the drudgery of compiling lists of names, titles, addresses, phone, fax, email and Web details by using the increasing number of information and contact companies that exist. They will supply ready-to-use databases of creative industry employee details available on CD or via email. The lists are ready-formatted for use in database software applications, such as Filemaker Pro, or can be simply supplied as printed envelope labels.

Although these services are not vastly expensive, for the lone illustrator starting out in the business they may be prohibitive. One approach can be to purchase one list at a time rather than hoping to hit all areas of the industry in the same marketing exercise. Often these companies produce separate lists for each of the design, book, newspaper and magazine publishing and advertising industries and these can be purchased separately. It is worth remembering that

Marketing

1. Postcards
Kenneth Andersson, 2004

2. Printed concertina promotional card, booklet and sticker
Jon Burgerman, 2004

3. Postcards and stickers
Jody Barton, 2004

The creation of marketing and promotional materials gives the illustrator the freedom to produce works that suggest at the content of their portfolio. Without necessarily having to communicate complex messages or content, the format can be chosen for personal preference or dictated by available budget. Some illustrators create a combination of printed materials and mail them together in a pack.

2.

3.

each database will have a best-before date of six months; most suppliers update their records every three months. A glance at the classified ads in the back pages of most prominent design and advertising magazines will detail any companies supplying contact information.

Cold-calling – making telephone calls to potential clients on the off-chance that they may have work or want to view a portfolio – is rarely successful. There was a time when magazine art directors and design company creative directors would put aside an afternoon each week to view portfolios and meet with freelance illustrators and photographers. Unfortunately, this magical slot appears to have disappeared in recent years, partly due to increased workloads, but also because other forms of self-promotion have become popular. Clients, after the initial contact has been made, are happy to converse on the phone, via email and to view images on screen from attachments or websites, so for many the face-to-face meeting has become a thing of the past.

Targeting

Promotional material arriving on the right desk of the right person is just one aspect of the self-promotion process. Ensuring that the most appropriate companies and organisations are targeted in the first place takes research and investigation. Understanding where, within the industry, your work will best fit is also important. There is little point in costly marketing to design companies specialising in corporate annual reports if you are a children's book illustrator, for example.

Research

Regular, straightforward research into potential clients can be done on a weekly or monthly basis without a huge inconvenience or expense. Keeping abreast of industry news and changes can be enjoyable, as well as productive. Visit a good library to read the wide range of monthly design and advertising press for information about specific commissions, as well as current projects being undertaken. This is the perfect way of gaining a broad knowledge of current industry trends. It is also possible to compile lists of art directors and designers working in magazines and newspapers from the information reproduced in publications.

1.

Mail-shots

Making the first contact with a potential client is important and creating the right impression is vital; the professional approach is to create a mail-shot that is simply posted to the recipient. Knowing what to send and how to package it is paramount to your mail-shot's success.

Postcards

Traditionally, illustrators produce postcards as samples of their work. They are relatively inexpensive to produce, cheap to send, and art directors and designers often have filing systems to accommodate them for future reference. Postcards are normally A6 in size, but a double-sized A5 card can look more professional. There are a vast number of print companies that have tapped into the market for producing postcards, many working exclusively for freelance photographers, models, actors and illustrators. Their rates can be reasonable as they 'gang up' the artwork, printing entire sheets of cards and not beginning production and print until they have collected enough artwork to fill the sheet.

Results can vary; some print companies will only supply a digital colour proof that will not give any information about the quality of the colour-match between the artwork and the final print. You tend to get what you pay for.

A successful way of creating well-printed cards on a good stock is to set up a group of illustrators and photographers – enough for an entire sheet – and approach independent printers with the job. Remember it will increase the workload for the person charged with

coordinating artwork, payments, preparing the digital files for the printer and ensuring that the deadline for delivery from each of the individual artists is met. Many illustration groups or collectives operate their own print programme to enable a steady and regular update of their printed publicity in exactly this manner.

Printed Promos

Postcards can leave some illustrators cold, believing that as creative individuals they should produce promotional materials in line with this – something more personal and memorable. It is true that other formats may interest and intrigue the viewer, but the life expectancy of the piece should be questioned. If it is too large to file with postcards, or to stick on to a wall or notice board, or if it is expected to take up valuable desk space, it is likely to be kept just hours rather than months. Every morning of every working day designers and art directors open their post, which mostly contains promotional materials from freelance creatives, and they make snap decisions about what to keep and what to bin.

If promotional material is to be effective, must grab the viewer's attention and present the facts and contact information in a clear, but interesting manner.

Ensuring the arrival of promotional material on the right desk of the right person is only one aspect of the self-promotion process.

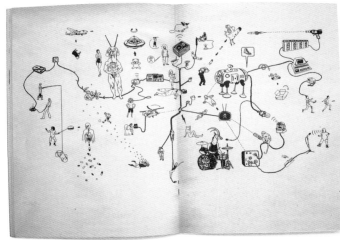

Marketing (II)

1. Various postcards and self-promotional button badge
NEW, 2003/05

2. Self-promotional book 'Perverted Science'
Andrew Rae, 2004

Producing a self-published promotional book is a large financial commitment, but in this example, created by Andrew Rae of Peepshow, the book also served as an exhibition catalogue for work he created for a group exhibition in London – dual usage ensured twice the potential audience coverage.

2.

Every morning of every working day designers and art directors open their post, which mostly contains promotional materials from freelance creatives, and they make snap decisions about what to keep and what to bin.

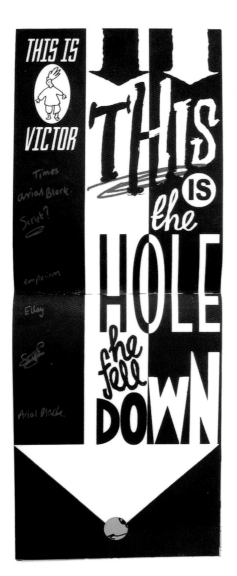

1.

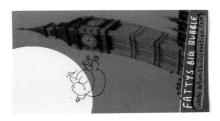

Marketing

• Marketing is a vital aspect of the illustrator's day-to-day regime. All successful illustrators must maintain a constant programme of mailing cards, brochures and stickers to keep attention and focus on their work.

• Sending real printed matter, rather than just emailing attachments, can still gain far more response from recipients. People in design, publishing and advertising like to see the real thing.

• Be creative and professional in your output and spend as much time and money as you can afford – this is an opportunity to create your best work, without the hindrance of a tight project brief.

• Use your marketing material to bring your work to the attention of those who you would most like to work for. If you aim to create openings in advertising, be sure to mail to art buyers, creative directors and art directors – they make the decisions about commissioning artists.

Marketing (III)

1. Screenprinted promotional book and cards
The Big Drop
Andy Smith, 2005

Creating impact and standing out from the crowd, an increasingly important aspect of marketing can be achieved in a variety of ways. Andy Smith produced a limited edition of 400 hand-numbered silk-screen printed books, along with a selection of cards that he mailed to potential clients.

Portfolios

Without a portfolio of work, the best publicity mail-out will be a wasted opportunity. The portfolio is the single most important asset that an illustrator needs to invest time, energy, attention to detail and finances in. Without a great portfolio working to your advantage, the next commission will be a long wait.

A portfolio may appear to be simply a selection of work in a binder of some description, but that assumption could cost an illustrator a dream project. To say that illustrators live and die by the strength of their portfolio is not an exaggeration. Whether tucked under your arm or tucked away on the Web, a great portfolio is essential.

Analogue Portfolios

Even in this digital age, real-world, real-time portfolios are still at the core of self-promotion.

Buying Guide

The first rule is to invest money in something that works well and looks the part. Using a battered plastic folio is fine if you are a student ferrying work back and forth from your room to art school studio. If you wish to be taken seriously, however, and aim to compete with the bigger fish, then you need to give your work the best possible presentation.

All good graphic-art material suppliers stock a range of products that will fit any budget, but spending money here is a good investment. A zipped, leather, ring-bound or loose-leaf book with perfectly clear translucent sleeves is not cheap, but it will stand the test of time and it will perform in an admirable fashion on your behalf. A good comfortable handle is important, as is a place to put your contact details on the outside of the book. A ring-bound book with sleeves will grow with you and adding more work becomes a simple process. Bear in mind that leather improves with age and plastic doesn't, and that getting the right size for your work is crucial too; if in doubt, seek advice in the shop. Remember, the portfolio is as important to the freelance illustrator as the limo is to the chauffeur, so this is not the time to economise.

Layout and Design

A great portfolio is only as good as the work within. Buying a fantastically expensive Italian leather folio will be a wasted investment if the work inside is not up to scratch. Making the right decisions on what to include and what to leave out is a tough call for a newcomer and expertise comes with practice and a little trial and error. Seek advice from clients, ask their opinions of your portfolio and adjust accordingly.

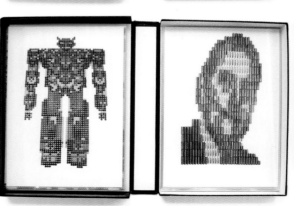

1.

Analogue Portfolios

1. Loose-leaf, presentation box portfolio
Ian Wright, 2005

Choosing the best format for a portfolio is paramount. Ian Wright, an established illustrator for over 20 years, chooses to display his work in loose sleeves within a professionally made presentation box. This allows him to tailor each presentation of the portfolio individually depending on the client and area of specialisation.

To say that illustrators live and die by the strength of their portfolio is not an exaggeration.

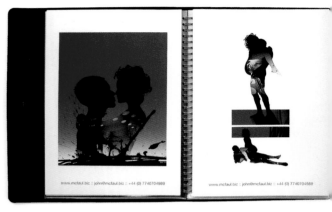

1.

'Show with your work that you can answer a brief and that you have a broad but individual style or way of working'.

Analogue Portfolio

1. Leather portfolio
McFaul, 2005

McFaul uses an illustration portfolio that has a leather cover and is spiral bound, enabling him to easily make adjustments to the running order of the work. Using high quality clear sleeves, kept in tip-top condition with lighter fuel and a soft cloth, McFaul ensures that his presentation is crisp, professional and succinct.

If in doubt about a particular piece of work, then you have already answered your own questioning mind. Only include work of which you are proud and can talk positively about in a meeting. Don't feel the need to include a project because your mother likes it, only those images that will work hard for you should be included. Put in work that demonstrates your strengths as an illustrator, that shows you can answer a brief and that you have a broad, but individual style or way of working.

Consider putting in work that demonstrates the context in which it was used; don't trim out your image but show the rest of the magazine page, for example, it will give the art director confidence if they can see that you already have been commissioned. Include work that gets you work; some pieces in a portfolio start to shine, watch for those that get the most attention or praise. Think carefully about the order that you place images in, start with a simple but bold and striking piece, perhaps one that people will recognise. Try to end on a similar feel and group images as you progress through the portfolio. Organise according to themes, colour, context or approaches – whatever best suits the work. Lay out images first in a large clear space – on your studio floor if clean – so that you can view all of them at once. Make decisions once you have tried a few variations, making lists on paper as you go so as to remember successful combinations.

It is very easy to include too much work or too little, and creating the right balance comes with experience. A general rule is to include ten to 15 sleeves, giving you room to show 20 to 30 images. Any more than this and some will never be viewed properly, just diluting the experience, any

less may leave the viewer wondering if you really can produce the goods.

Consider carefully how you plan and 'design' the layout; for example, an A3 portfolio looks best when only one image is used per page. Don't crowd a page; leaving space around an image gives it a chance to 'breath' and it can be absorbed more easily without the visual distraction of other images. Use the same colour backing-sheet throughout the portfolio; consistency works best in this instance. Resist the temptation to window-mount images, it always looks over-laboured and unnecessary.

Labels can be added to each page, if helpful to the viewer, but ensure that they work well typographically. Keep the type simple and use an uncluttered font such as a sans-serif face like Ariel or Helvetica. Range the type to the left and allow for a margin of space around the edge. Place the caption in a standard position on each sleeve, keep the descriptions short and use the same format throughout the portfolio.

Maintenance and Upkeep

Getting a portfolio up and running is only part of the solution, keeping it looking good and performing well is a regular task that needs constant attention. Clean portfolio sleeves with a wipe of lighter fuel on a cotton cloth, replace damaged ones and carefully reposition images that have come unstuck and shifted. All this takes very little time, but can be easily overlooked.

Updating on a regular basis, adding new work and taking out older pieces is necessary to maintain your portfolio's effectiveness. The portfolio may need an entire overhaul as the addition or

replacement of just a few images can put the whole running order out of sync. A portfolio really should be this exact.

Your Portfolio

• Keep track of exactly where your portfolio is. Label it on the outside with all your contact details.

• Despatch departments are often responsible for returning your portfolio, make sure your return info is presented clearly.

• Stock portfolios with portfolio samples to keep, the client may only remember your work on the strength of these.

• A duplicate portfolio prevents loss of earnings when the original is held up elsewhere.

• Feature your experimental illustrations at the back of your portfolio, and caption clearly. A good art director will want to see aspects of any shift in approach. It can also be a great talking point.

When preparing a portfolio to be sent out to a client, it is always wise to check that it's in good shape. Fine-tuning the selection to suit the viewer or the potential job that it has been called in for is the next logical step. It is better to have a few more examples of book jackets than CD sleeve designs if the portfolio is going into the art department of a publishing company, for example.

Good Practice

Put samples and publicity material in the rear pocket so that art directors and designers have access to a permanent record of your work after a viewing. Make sure that all your contact details are easily visible on the outside of your folio. This is crucial in order to have your book returned by any courier.

For those illustrators that are kept constantly busy with work, setting up an account with a local courier company is a useful asset. Being able to make a call, without any hiccups or problems, to a company that can be relied upon when an urgent request for a portfolio comes saves a lot of time and stress.

Portfolio insurance is another worthwhile consideration; not all courier companies are reliable and there are many instances of portfolios going astray within large organisations. Again, although not cheap, insurance should be a consideration for those that have portfolios constantly moving across town or are sending them abroad, something that is occurring more and more often.

Creating duplicates of your portfolio can be incredibly useful if you are in demand. Losing a job because your book can't be sent to the client, as it is sitting in another office somewhere on the other side of town, is very frustrating but will happen. Creating more than one portfolio is expensive, but a single editorial job will easily pay for it and for the working professional, being ready, prepared and organised must be second nature.

Finally, be a little experimental; add pieces of personal work to the last few sleeves of your portfolio. It is advisable to caption them so that the viewer understands that they are non-commissioned artworks. Showing examples of new ways of working will sit well against the rest of the portfolio of completed and finished projects, and it will demonstrate how your work is creatively developing. If you are present when your portfolio is viewed, be positive and be proud. You need to do your portfolio justice and vice-versa.

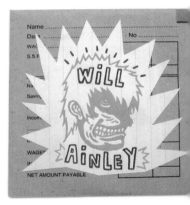

1.

2.

Digital Portfolios

No longer just an added extra to the leather-bound portfolio but increasingly just as important, the digital equivalent requires planning, foresight, imagination and an appreciation for the viewer's perspective.

Slide Shows

Slide shows are easy to build and use, and are readily available. Search the Web for freeware applications that run simple slide show presentations or purchase one that does the job, but is inexpensive. Dragging a small digital file on to an open application is as complex as the experience gets. Editing the running order, the time given for each image to appear on screen and simple commands to adjust the transition or dissolve between each image, is likely to be the full extent of any design considerations. This is enough for a professional-looking presentation. Slide shows can be burnt on to CD and emailed.

A key aspect of these types of software applications is that they run independently, they do not require the host computer to have the software pre-installed. This ensures that any machine is capable of viewing the presentation without technical difficulties.

Presentation Software

Microsoft's PowerPoint and Apple's Keynote are both pieces of software that can be designed to run with little or no involvement by the viewer. This is ideal for those choose to create more structured presentations than slide show software will accommodate. Type can be added, allowing for captions that identify the images or for titling at the start and end of the show. Contact details can also be created and added, as well as copyright, infringement notices.

Good presentation software allows for animation and film to be run directly from the application, allowing for a more accomplished overall look if moving image projects make up an aspect of the portfolio.

These formats have a second use in the purpose of publicity too. The main advantage over printed material is that the initial financial outlay is considerably less. Allowing for constant change and updating, these formats enable ease of creation for a specific audience or client and can potentially showcase many more images than a traditional leather-bound book.

The price of a CD, an envelope and the postage stamps combined is far less than a courier bill for the same distance journey and financial demands do not dictate that the CD is returned. This is a workable portfolio that acts well as a publicity and marketing tool as well.

3.

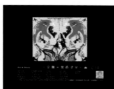

4.

Digital Portfolio

• Create any digital presentation in up-to-the-minute software applications that can be read by both PC and Macintosh platforms.

• Test your presentation on various computers and screens to view as your client will see it – do this before you start making copies.

• Stock portfolios with portfolio samples to keep as the client may only remember your work on the strength of these.

• Ask your regular clients if they respond to this type of presentation – new media companies and animation and production houses will be quite used to viewing work in this format – book publishers will not be.

• Make the experience of viewing your digital portfolio a user-friendly one. Potential clients will not hang around waiting for your presentation to start, nor will they continue if the navigation is complex or unusable instantly.

Digital Portfolios

1. Web-based portfolio screenshots
Will Ainley, 2005

2. CD-Rom and CD sleeve
Will Ainley, 2005

Combining printed medium, and traditional postage methods, with new media – a Web-based off-line portfolio – can create results that span both analogue and digital avenues. Will Ainley, a young illustrator with just a few years' experience out of college, utilises 'found' envelopes to add a collaged effect to his promotional material – it fits visually with his working method.

3. Printed promotional poster with CD-Rom
CIA, 2004

4. Screenshots of digital portfolio from Agency Digital Presentation
CIA, 2004

CIA, Central Illustration Agency, with offices in London and New York produced an innovative fold-out poster as a promotional item. The poster, with just a few simple cuts at the finishing stage, houses a CD-Rom presentation of work by the artists that the agency represents.

The Website

A website is a must have. Luckily, it is not a necessary start-up tool and can be added to the armoury a little later as a career starts to develop. Getting a website working in a useful and meaningful way, takes vision and an understanding of the medium.

Before you even start to consider your own website, research plenty of sites by other illustrators first. Start by getting URLs from illustration organisations; the Association of Illustrators in London has links to its members' sites. Gather more links from details published in annuals and Google-search for direct access to sites. Learn from how others use the Web as a medium for housing a portfolio before embarking upon your own.

Establish who is going to design your site; if you are doing it yourself, make sure that you set yourself realistic goals and a time-frame to produce the work in. Investigate employing a Web designer, they will have far more experience and bring expertise to the project – perhaps a recent graduate just entering the profession and looking to broaden his or her own portfolio. Friends that are designers may be interested in trading artworks for website work, so be up front and ask.

Content

Consider the content of your site before embarking on its look and feel. Think carefully about the job that you would like the site to accomplish. If purely a portfolio site, it may just contain images and captions but it could be a missed opportunity.

Other content to include might be a short welcome introduction and then a brief biography including some information about your education, recent projects, upcoming exhibitions etc. Work out how to group your work into sections; all editorial commissions could be in one area, book covers and design company projects in another. Having an area that is used to showcase new and uncommissioned work can be instrumental in allowing others to see the direction that new work is taking.

1.

Websites

1. Drag-and-drop
www.spencerwilson.co.uk
Spencer Wilson, 2005

One option for displaying work samples is to use drag-and-drop. By highlighting and dragging an image into the centre of the screen it automatically opens a new image.

2. Pop-up windows
www.mediumphobic.com
Nicholas Di Genova, 2004
designed by Studio ThoughtCrimez

One option for displaying work samples is to use pop-up windows. These can be activated from small 'thumbnails' that once clicked, launch larger windows that sit independently from the browser window.

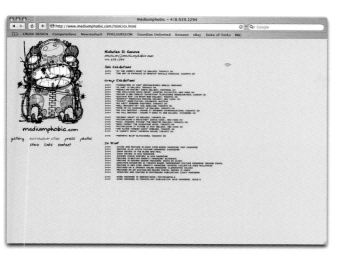

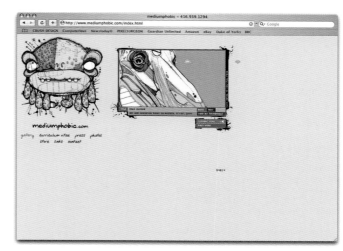

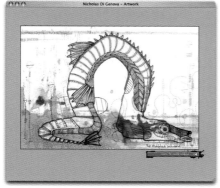

Websites

• If you are not a keen Web designer, why take the time and energy to learn new software that you'll probably not need to use again? Look to trade your skills for those of a good Web designer – offer some specially commissioned illustrations or even one-off artworks as incentive.

• Sit down and plan your site carefully, looking at many other illustrator's sites first – find what you think works well and avoid mistakes that others have made before you.

• Consider your audience – a basic CV and/or Biog will be enough professional and personal information for most clients. Avoid the temptation to tell your entire life history, so keep to the relevant facts – education, exhibitions, client list etc.

• Caption your work samples. Give information about each piece of work – client, brief description of project, title and medium created in. This will ensure that the viewer reads your images as commissioned illustrations rather than just abstract images out-of-context.

2.

Easy access to your contact details is important, although it is safest to only publish email contact info – remember you are unable to control exactly who can view your site. Another useful area of content is a page containing links to other websites that you recommend. Links from your site to others may mean that they also provide links back to your site, thus increasing the amount of potential traffic. It is advisable to make contact before creating a link, this will ensure that a link back is considered too.

Some illustrators find that the extra-curricular work of creating limited-edition digital or screenprints, or even a small range of T-shirts can be successfully marketed on a website and start to form the basis for a small on-line shop. It is unlikely that business demands will ever overflow into a major commitment, but there may be enough interest to warrant time and finances being directed towards a shop as part of the overall presence being created.

Design, Navigation and Layout

The best advice for those working on their first site is to keep things simple. Nothing is more disconcerting or off-putting than a badly designed website that is difficult to navigate. Map out a simple diagram of the basic structure before work on the site begins. Identify each of the separate areas as a box and link each box with lines to show how the viewer will navigate the site. It may well take numerous attempts to complete the diagram, but the exercise will ensure that questions regarding content and structure are raised, if not truly answered, at this stage.

The overall design of the site needs addressing soon after the structure diagram has been resolved. Knowing how the site will look and feel early on will be an advantage, resolving design considerations is easiest early on in a project. The design should compliment the illustration work it houses and not distract the viewer from the work. Keep text to a minimum, as most people don't enjoy scrolling through pages and pages of copy on-screen. Create captions to identify the work's key points and ensure all images sit comfortably on screen without any need for scrolling.

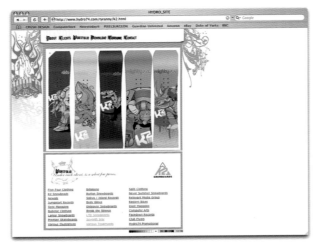

 1.

Think about the route that viewers will take when accessing all aspects of your site and make sure that no area takes more than a few clicks of the mouse to get to.

Website

1. On-line portfolio
www.hydro74.com
Joshua Smith, 2005

Working predominately for surf, skate and snowboard clients in a youth sector of the market, Joshua Smith, based in Florida, uses his website to showcase recent commissions and projects, as well as providing downloadable free vector images and fonts.

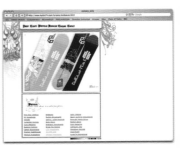

Navigation should be easy to use without being too childishly obvious. Ensure that all areas of the site can be reached without the need for the viewer to leave to use the 'back' button of the Web browser. Think about the route that viewers will take when accessing all aspects of your site and make sure that no area takes more than a few clicks of the mouse to get to. People want to access information quickly with the minimum of fuss.

Although most users will have fast connections to the Internet, some will not and this needs to be taken into account when considering content. Make sure that pages download quickly by keeping the file sizes for images small and don't add unnecessary animated details for the sake of it.

Maintenance, Upkeep and Promotion

Just as a real-world portfolio needs constant attention, so does an on-line version. Keeping the site up to date with new work and forthcoming exhibitions and events is crucial and should not be too time-consuming. Checking that the site views well on a range of different machines, screens and different browsers is part of the development process, but

should be checked periodically once up and running as well.

A website that is not promoted effectively is about as useful as having no website at all. Promotion can be as simple as ensuring that 'keywords' are embedded in the front page; this is where search engines look for information about a site and identify what it contains. Using a range of keywords will help broaden the appeal to search engines but be realistic; the word 'illustrator' reveals over three million results in Google, whereas 'editorial illustrator, New York,' limits the search to 100,000.

Promoting your site with a postcard mailed through the post may seem like a backwards step technologically, but can really increase awareness and traffic. Emailing a link to your site and including some low-res images will increase awareness too. Without an audience a website will just sit on the hard shoulder of the information superhighway without any place to go.

Both analogue and digital portfolios are the lifeblood of the working illustrator, without them working hard on your behalf, it can be impossible to win even the first commission.

Website

2. Structure planning diagram

Before embarking upon the design yourself or commissioning the design of your website, start by making a sketch or diagram that highlights the main areas of the site. By working out the structure beforehand, you'll get a real sense of how the user will navigate through your site. Ensure that the route that they'll take is easy to follow – nothing is more frustrating than spending ages attempting to find information that is hidden away in hard-to-find places. Keep your site succinct, but with enough detail to interest the user – don't over-complicate. The site should promote your work as an illustrator, not your skills nor your designer's skills as a Web designer.

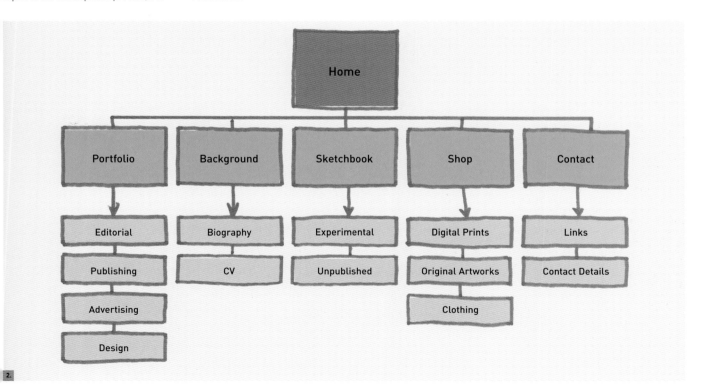

2.

Avenues for Self-Promotion

The self-promoting illustrator should plan to make an impact that leads to a request to view a portfolio of work, with or without the illustrator present, a decision to click on a website for more illustration samples, or even directly commission work. Publicity is never created with the intention of securing a job for life or to set out an in-depth professional history or profile, so simplicity is the key. It is never wise to send a long resume or CV: it should be the quality of the work that dictates the approach. Many art school graduates are pleased to announce just where they studied and what degree they got, and are frustrated when they realise that it is purely the quality of the portfolio of work that interests the viewer.

Creating an annual desktop or wall-mounted calendar, for example, can work as an effective promotional device; they are useful objects as well as a daily reminder of the illustrator's work. Remember though, that every print company, photographic agency, stock-image library and facilities house will have the same idea and probably bigger budgets, so that on the first Monday of January every art director in town will spend most of the morning opening large, well-sealed envelopes with calendars inside. Christmas is never a good time for sending out publicity. Although it may be a time for giving, Christmas is not a time for receiving commissions and any promotional material sent out then will be land-fill by January.

Pop-up or stand-up promo pieces that are intended to attract attention as desktop novelties invariably don't stand the test of time. Objects that require construction will probably remain unbuilt. Creating a device that works well, that inspires, surprises or raises a smile will, however, produce results. Clients like to be impressed, are flattered and will appreciate the time and energy involved in creating a promotional item that communicates effectively. Illustrators that create posters, boxes of images, concertina hand-made books and any number of elaborate promo objects inevitably receive requests to visit with a portfolio of work. The secret is in creating a promotional object that is well-targeted, well-designed and well worth receiving.

The Annuals

Annuals offer another distinct area of investigation in the search for self-promotional nirvana. There are three different types that illustrators can aspire to have their work included in and all do the job, albeit in slightly different ways.

The first, and definitely the most aspirational of the three, is the annual of work that has been selected and judged by distinguished industry peers. These annuals are compiled and published by organisations like the Society of Illustrators in New York and the Association of Illustrators in London, and are normally launched at an exhibition of work from the book. The SOI in New York was founded in 1901 and has published over 47 annuals, simply entitled 'Illustrators', whilst the AOI in London, formed in 1973, has published 28 editions of its annual, 'Images'.

There is stiff competition in every category for entry to the SOI and AOI annuals each year. For many, the call for entries has become something of an annual ritual, despite never knowing what may catch the judges' eyes to make it into the final selection, and there is never a shortage of those hoping to make it into the book and accompanying exhibition.

The second category of annual also works as a full-colour index of illustrators' work and contact details, but there is a fee for entry. These are normally determined by a page rate, and it is this fact that identifies the annual as being more representative of the entire industry rather than the best of the work being produced. These annuals show work to suit all tastes, but not all of it will be very good.

The third type of annual is more restrictive as entry is entirely reserved for illustration agents to book pages in. This has benefits for those that use the annual; they know that each and every illustrator featured can be contacted through their agents. Many clients like to deal only through an agency, but more on that issue later in this chapter.

Annuals can be expensive to enter, only appear once a year and can give the impression of a creative cattle market, but they do have one major benefit that outweighs any negative perceptions. Annuals are distributed free of charge to those in the industry who commission illustration; they are sent to advertising agencies, book publishers and design companies, and are always kept and referred to. Targeting and reaching this broad an audience in one hit with a professional piece of promotion is never easy, and for this reason alone inclusion in an annual is a must.

Another reason to consider the annual is their run-ons. A run-on is exactly what it sounds like; exact copies of individual pages of the book printed as extra, one-sided sheets. As a useful incentive for inclusion, the publishers of the annuals build into the price supplying 500–1000 run-ons of the artist's page into the overall cost. This means that the individual illustrator then has a ready-made piece of publicity for marketing purposes.

Targeting and reaching this broad an audience in one hit with a professional piece of promotion is never easy, and for this reason alone inclusion in an annual is a must.

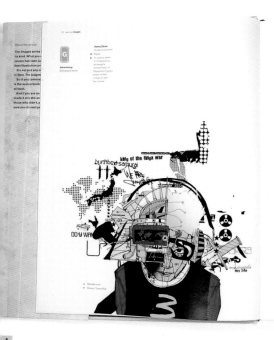

1.

Judged Annuals

1. Images 28
The Association of Illustrators, 2004

2. Illustrators 45
The Society of Illustrators, 2003

Peer- or industry-judged annuals are deemed to carry the most weight professionally. Annuals published by the AOI in the UK and the SOI in the US have a ready-made audience looking for both new and established talent.

2.

1.

Pay and Display Annuals

1. Le Book
Le Book Publishing, 2004

2. Contact 2004
Contact Publishing, 2004

To guarantee entry into an annual, opt for the pay-and-display option – normally published within the first quarter of a new calendar year and mailed directly to all top industry companies on your behalf. Expensive, if you pay the rate-card price, but your work is included along with everyone else that has paid – good work and bad.

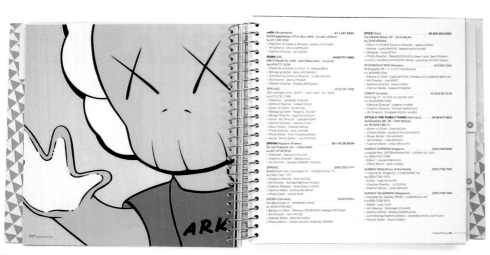

2.

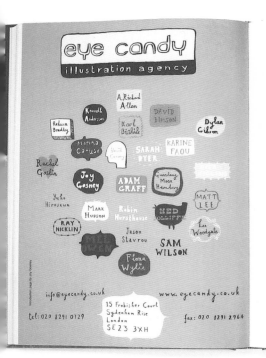

Annuals

• Three different annuals that at first glance - look alike. Judged annuals carry the most weight with agency-only coming in a close second. However there are genuine bonuses to the Pay-and-display type – guaranteed entry.

• Check what the final price will be for each annual. Judged annuals carry a fee for entry and also for selection – read the small print carefully. Fees for the agency-only annual should be split between yourself and your agent – how the percentages are cut should be agreed before you contribute. Pay-and-display annuals display their rates on promotional material – ask for a discount as they want your business!

• Deadlines vary for each type of annual. It is worth remembering that lead times for judged annuals will be quite lengthy – you may submit work to be judged a good six to eight months before the book is published, so choose your submission carefully as this piece will represent you for a further 12 months if chosen.

Agency-Only Annuals

3. 'The Art Book 2004'
John Pigeon Publishing, 2004

Some annuals cater only for illustration agencies to contribute work on behalf of their represented artists. Some clients prefer this approach, seeking to make contact solely through an agent, ensuring a risk-free commissioning process.

3.

Illustration Agency Representation

If the whole idea of maintaining a strong marketing and publicity campaign, keeping mailing lists up-to-date, coordinating the delivery as well as the upkeep of your portfolios seems unmanagable then it may be wise to consider approaching an illustration agency for representation.

Agencies are a useful link to the professional world for those illustrators that are either too busy to spend time undertaking the business side of the discipline, find that they are just not very good at it or do not enjoy meeting new clients on a regular basis. Having an external 'face' is an exceptionally useful tool for many so that for this, and other contributing factors, artists are prepared to shed a percentage of their fee for the service.

The Positive Aspects

Debate about the relative pros and cons of agency representation continue to surface, but for those happily housed within an agency portfolio, most of the issues are positive. Being able to hand over the financial negotiations of a project to someone often far more adept and practiced can be a real relief for some. Having an agent involved in quoting a fee for a potential or real project can increase the final fee; many illustrators have issues understanding the marketplace and exactly what their work is worth. It is not uncommon for an agency to command and receive fees over and above the illustrator's own perception of what the fee should be. This can mean that agency representation can pay for itself; an agent who can charge 25% higher fees than a solo artist is, indirectly, creating their own percentage from a project.

Good agents relate to their client base, they know their market and fully understand the business of illustration. The best agents have spent time building relationships with art directors, art buyers and designers and are on friendly terms

➡

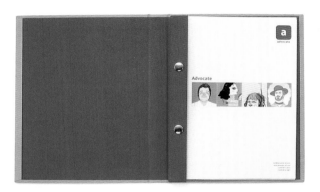

1.

Agency Representation

1. Advocate art portfolio
Advocate Art, 2005

2. 'CIA Quarterly'
CIA, 2005

Professional presentation and promotion should be guaranteed with representation by an established illustration agency. Time, effort and financial backing ensure marketing tools are created that reflect an agency's approach to business. Well-designed and well-considered, great marketing can attract work an individual illustrator would struggle to find on their own.

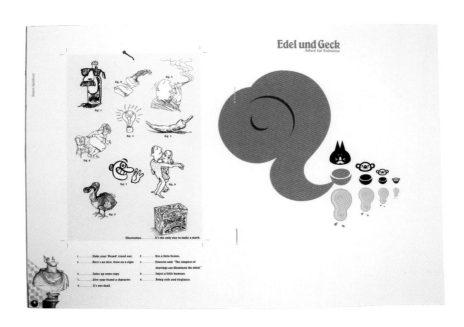

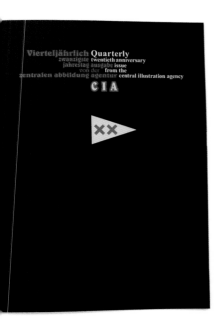

2.

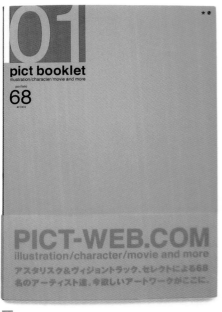

1.

with them. Clients trust good agents, as they seek advice about the most appropriate artist for a particular project. The agent can be the first person called when a commission is forthcoming. Some agents have been in the business for many years and have established themselves as experts in the field – this is not easy to replicate as a solo artist.

Most agencies share the burden and cost of publicity with their artists, a rule-of-thumb being that an agency pays the same percentage towards the costs as the percentage that they take in fees. Some will pay for one major agency publicity publication each year in addition, but each company has its own take on what they offer. Many artists, when the relationship works well, find that most work starts to come through the agency and so feel less of a need for their own self-promotional material. This, in itself, can be a huge release.

Agencies deliver portfolios and quote on potential projects. Both tasks can be time-consuming and will not generate income unless developing into real commissions. Illustrators running their own business affairs can waste much time chasing jobs that don't happen. The artist often overlooks this aspect of agency representation, but it is this job that is the foundation of an agency's success and reputation.

Agency representation also means the artist avoids the task of chasing up purchase orders and paperwork related to a project. Producing detailed invoices with tight information about the parameters of the usage of a particular artwork can be no fun to work out either. Constantly phoning accounts departments after 30 days to enquire why an invoice remains unpaid is a weary and soul-destroying task and an efficient agent takes care of all this.

The Negative Aspects

Not all aspects of agency representation appeal to every artist though. Illustration agencies are businesses, and in order to stay in business they must represent artists that are in fashion and will win commissions. Agencies are less likely to take creative risks when considering new artists and this can have the effect of stifling the industry by ignoring emerging new talents.

Agents will expect artists interested in joining them to already have a substantial back catalogue and a regular supply of new work. Even with this, they may demand that an artist works solely through the agency and hand over all client details at the start of the arrangement. Another real drawback can be that not all clients are prepared to work with agents, some have a reputation

for being hard-nosed, demanding unreasonable fees and will only work directly with artists.

Issues of communication are in the forefront of some minds and many prefer to keep the lines of communication as short as possible. An agent may be seen as another link in a chain that can so easily lead to game of Chinese Whispers.

Whatever the ups and downs of agents and the roles that they play, it is wise to get first-hand knowledge and experience. If looking for an agent, aim to meet with as many as possible, send in samples to agencies that best suit your own approach and methods of work. Seek advice from illustrators that are represented, look at the range and depth of the illustrators already with agencies that interest you. Be prepared and be knowledgeable. If you are talented, it is likely that more than one agency will be interested in representing you; don't go with the first offer, consider them all and then decide.

Being able to hand over the financial negotiations of a project to someone often far more adept and practiced can be a real relief for some.

Agency Representation

1. Promotional literature
Pict

Japanese agency, Pict, promote its stable of artists within a full-colour promotional book. Each artist is given a full page and a brief description of their approach. Volume 01 was so successful it was decided to publish Volume 02 in larger numbers, assign it an ISBN number and sell through independent art and design book stores, as well as mail to Pict's client list.

2. CIA playing cards
Central illustration agency

Quirky promotional materials really do stand out – a limited edition set of playing cards created by CIA became a highly sought-after item. Artists were proud to have contributed to a unique and successful promotional device and clients were more than happy to receive it. Projects such as this elevate the status of an agency.

Agency Representation – Pros

• Agents are unafraid to demand the best possible fees. They don't get embarrassed – the higher the fee, the bigger their percentage.

• Although agents can command between 20%–30% of the final fee as their own – they are likely to gain a higher fee than a lone illustrator could.

• Some advertising agents will only deal with artists through their agent – no agent can mean no work for some companies.

• Agents have experience of managing careers – they can advise you what direction to consider taking your work in. They see many more portfolios than you ever can.

• Many illustrators hate having to attend meetings – they don't enjoy the process and agents willingly take on this burden of responsibility.

Agency Representaion – Cons

• Some clients refuse to work through agencies – they want direct contact with the illustrator they wish to work with – believing that the best work is produced with a shorter chain.

• There are clients that begrudge paying the higher fees that an agent may command – they see agents as mercenaries!

• The financial pressure to maintain high-profile marketing can be too expensive, as well as being creatively limiting for some illustrators. Many prefer to set their own personal direction for marketing and publicity.

• Some agents demand that all work goes through the agency – meaning that a percentage of the fees from regular work from contacts and clients built up over time is liable to be paid to the agent.

• Not all illustrators trust agents – having a businessman tackle issues of creativity whilst acting as a middleman just seems inappropriate to some.

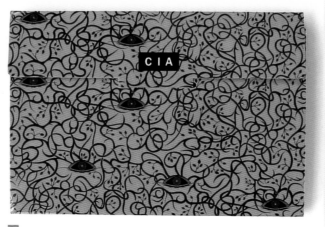

2.

Seek advice from illustrators that are represented, and look at the range and depth of the illustrators already with agencies that interest you.

1. Promotional literature
Pearce Stoner Associates

An agency's promotional material designed to serve dual purposes will ensure full value for money. Here, Pearce Stoner Associates has created a set of cards that can be mailed individually or included in an artist's portfolio, but when punched and tied together creates an effective agency book.

1.

Presentation Techniques

Whether with an agent or working solo, you will have to spend time making many presentations to clients on a regular basis, starting from the point of that very first meeting.

Presentation techniques are no mystery, but can prove problematic for some artists. Despite an art school training that can require constant justification of a piece of work, often in group situations, many illustrators do not communicate clearly in meetings with their own clients.

It is important to be confident about your work when presenting your portfolio, although there is a fine line between confidence and arrogance; show self-belief and be positive about what you do and how you work. A friendly manner is much more appealing than a cool stand-off nature, as many clients choose whom to work with based on personality as much as portfolio work.

Speak slowly and clearly, and aim to perform during a review of your portfolio or when you present visuals or final artwork to a client. It is wise to remember a few short background stories behind one or two pieces of work. Clients may view your work and meet with you in a busy studio, if a meeting room is unavailable. Don't let this phase you. You may be interrupted by others in the studio asking questions or phones ringing. Try to take it all in your stride and be professional; sulking or storming out will get you nowhere.

Demonstrate enthusiasm for your client's business as well as your own, and research the company that you are meeting with; look at recent projects and be able to ask questions and make comments that show you are knowledgeable about their work and current issues too. At the same time, be aware of the need to listen, as when nervous it is easy to talk too much, if you find yourself in this situation try to slow down and take stock.

Don't be afraid to take notes, as it is better to have something on paper to refer to after the meeting. With the possibility of so much information being relayed in a relatively short space of time, it is very easy to forget key aspects. Take a notepad and pen and start the meeting with them to hand.

Do ensure that you look professional: the design and advertising worlds are fairly relaxed and informal environments, but it is important to look and feel appropriately dressed. Personal hygiene should not be an issue for discussion, being clean and tidy must be a given. Some meetings will require a business suit; a presentation of final artwork to the end client of a project is a case in point. Just like the extra duplicate portfolio that sits in the studio, having a change of clothes ready, in case of an urgent meeting can be a blessing.

Overall, it is important to be yourself, but a confident, approachable and motivated version. Switch it on when you enter a meeting, if need be; it can and will make a difference.

Personal hygiene should not be an issue for discussion, being clean and tidy must be a given.

2.

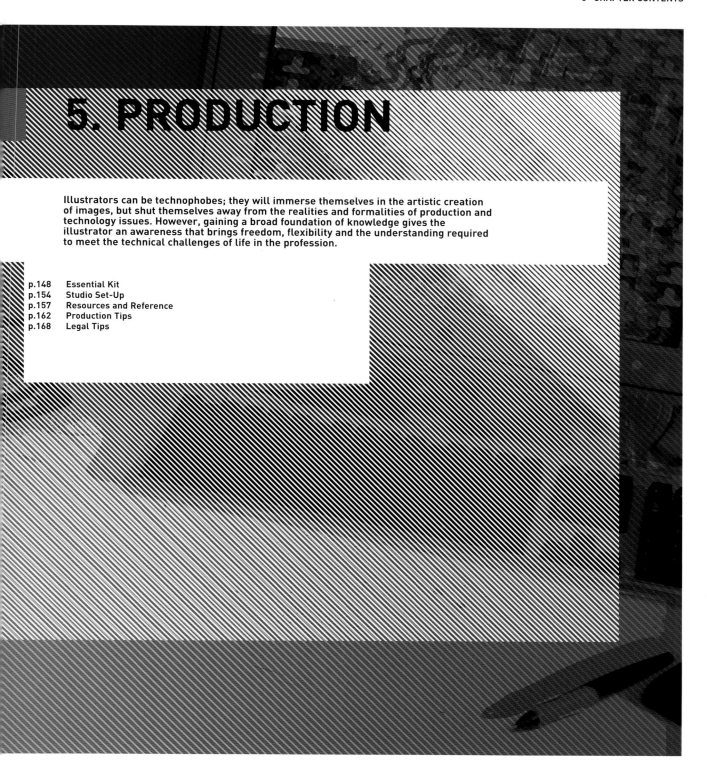

5. PRODUCTION

Illustrators can be technophobes; they will immerse themselves in the artistic creation of images, but shut themselves away from the realities and formalities of production and technology issues. However, gaining a broad foundation of knowledge gives the illustrator an awareness that brings freedom, flexibility and the understanding required to meet the technical challenges of life in the profession.

Essential Kit

As previously discussed, illustrators work in a variety and combination of different media and most start to find the materials that they feel an affinity for during the latter part of their art and design education. A growing understanding of how materials behave is part of that journey, but an aspect missing in the education programmes of many design institutions is that of in-depth teaching of production issues. In order to discuss these demands, it is important to start with the basic components and materials that illustrators use daily in the studio.

Basics

Find the materials that work for you. Try a range of products and brands, but be clear which ones give you the results that you are happy with. There is no top brand of acrylic paint, no definitive make of pencil; there are only the materials that you work best with. Whether working with spray paint and finding that a particular nozzle works in the most satisfying way, or discovering that a certain squeegee drags the ink in a more effective manner, it is about choice.

Trial and error are crucial to discovering the right tools and materials. Learn to follow instinct and don't be afraid to ask the opinions of others. Be prepared to give some materials the benefit of the doubt as not many can be mastered in minutes and most need time to adjust working methods to them. When you find a specific brush or shade of paint that works, it can be a heart-warming moment. The same feeling can be felt when an aspect of a software application is mastered, and you correctly perform a task that moves a piece of work forward in a new direction. ➡

7.

8.

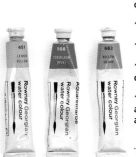

9.

Analogue Essentials

1. Pencils with leads of various thickness

2. Coloured pencils

3. Wax crayons in various colours

4. White lettering chalk for use on dark or black paper

5. Paintbrushes of various bristle widths

6. Long-handled dip pen with nib

7. Inks in various colours

8. Long sticks of willow charcoal

9. Cellulose thinners used to thin certain paints and for transfer of images to paper

10. Aerosol paint in various colours

11. Oil pastels in various colours

12. Paint, mainly available in acrylic, oil, poster and watercolour

13. Marker pens in various widths and colours using permanent and semi-permanent inks

There are no best brands, there are no certain winners – only the materials and tools that best suit your working methods. By experimenting with these tools and others available, new, unexpected uses may be discovered, leading to unique, process-based techniques that are truly personal to the illustrator.

10.

11.

12.

13.

The joy is in understanding how the combination and mix of materials can give very different results.

It is rare to find a shop that sells all the right products under one roof and it can take visits to various shops to find the places that sell the particular type, brand or range that you require. There is something about the atmosphere of a good art supply shop that evokes feelings of excitement and awe, like a child in a sweet shop. Shopping on-line is time-saving and convenient, but can be a sterile experience. Wandering the aisles of Pearl Paint off Canal Street, in New York, the London Graphic Centre in Covent Garden or Tokyu Hands in the Shinjuku district of Tokyo is an experience that can't be replicated on-screen.

There are some items of kit that have simply been essential must-haves for the illustrator since the discipline's birth. There are others that have become essential in recent years with the advent and introduction of digital working methods.

Analogue Essentials

Even for the digital artist, paper is normally the starting point. Paper comes in a multitude of formats, weights and finishes and the choice of stock is dependent on the usage. There is little point in attempting to use watercolour paints in a bleed-proof marker pad, common sense is the overruling factor most of the time.

All artists understand, or rapidly find out, the difference between a hard and soft lead in a pencil, how to fix a charcoal drawing on location or the benefits of a putty rubber over an office eraser; the trick is in adapting the materials to suit the user.

Digital Essentials

It is now impossible to consider an illustrator successfully working without access to digital tools, an idea unthinkable even at the end of the 20th century. Whether an artist creates all work on-screen or scans in original drawings to be reworked or coloured in the computer, or they simply attach final artworks into emails to deliver to the client, almost every aspect of the process can be digitised.

When considering the purchase of digital equipment it pays, yet again, to seek advice. It is rare to be in the position of an all-encompassing equipment purchase in one dramatic sweep of the computer store; most people tend to buy what they need as and when they require it, updating and upgrading as they go. Most students will

The joy is in understanding how the combination and mix of materials can give very different results, and how to be unafraid of the challenge of experimentation.

1.

2.

3.

4.

5.

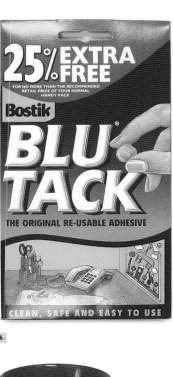

6.

7.

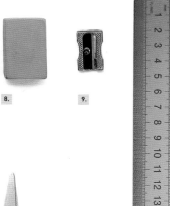

8.

9.

10.

11.

12.

13.

14.

15.

16.

Analogue Essentials (II)

1. Multi-purpose artist's tape

2. Brown tape used for stretching paper

3. Circle Cutter

4. Rub-down letters for applying type to analogue artwork

5. Stencils for hand-rendered type

6. Sticky putty for positioning and repositioning elements within a collage

7. Masking tape for sticking and repositioning

8. A putty rubber is a good quality pencil eraser

9. Pencil sharpener

10. PVA glue for paper sticking and for adding to acrylic paint to make it opaque

11. Spray adhesive for accurate control when gluing

12. Good quality paper scissors

13. A steel rule avoids the damage a scalpel would do to a plastic ruler

14. Glue stick – useful for quick and easy paper sticking (although often not permanent enough for artwork usage)

15. Medical Scalpel for excellent cutting control

16. Medical scalpel blades for use in conjunction with scalpel – 10A blades are the most multi-purpose

have used equipment made available during their studies and will find on graduating that they have to purchase some kit for the first time.

Speaking to other illustrators and getting recommendations pays dividends. There is very little point in buying a top spec, high-end computer that is capable of rendering 3D graphics in seconds at a huge cost if you work in watercolour and only intend to use the machine to send artwork via email and conduct Web-based research.

The Computer

Basic digital requirements will always include a computer and the biggest decisions will always start with making the choice between buying a PC or Apple Mac and choosing between desktop or laptop. Personal preference will dictate which route is taken, but considering a portable machine is worthwhile. Being able to work at the studio and in the home, as well as working and making presentations on the move, is a major bonus. Laptop computers can be locked away overnight to avoid theft and can be plugged into large desktop monitors when a larger working area is needed. They may have less raw power than a desktop model, but for most illustrators they are more than adequate.

The Scanner

A scanner to input hand-drawn images and found printed reference into the computer is essential, although a small A4 version is all that is normally needed. For those who aim to draw directly into a software application, a drawing tablet is essential kit. They can take a little time to master fully, but many experienced digital illustrators swear by them.

The Printer

Outputting images on a digital printer is important when keeping a portfolio up to date, but far less important as a tool for checking colours. The process that a budget digital printer goes through in creating colours for print is very different from the four-colour printing process used in industrial off-set lithography used by publishers.

The Camera

A good digital camera is a must, both as a useful tool for inputting images, and for shooting reference material. Being able to capture the figure in various poses to then bring into an application for drawing or retouching makes figure work much less time-consuming and less dependent on traditional skills.

A recent upsurge in vector-drawn and traced figures in illustrations in recent years has been directly brought about by the relative simplicity of this process.

Backing Up

Backing up, storing and archiving work is a boring, but necessary aspect of digital work. It can take some freelancers a major computer crash and loss of files before they are ready to begin a pattern of regular back-ups. Although wise to copy work files on to an external hard drive, these are not indestructible and must not be regarded as completely error-free places to archive work. A small drive that fits in a bag or pocket is better value per megabyte than a small keyring USB storage device, but it is also vital to back up on to CD or DVD and create duplicate copies of each disc too. Get into the habit of keeping one set of data in an alternative location; it is best to be thorough before the inevitable occurs.

It is impossible nowadays to consider an illustrator working without access to digital tools, an idea unthinkable even towards the end of the last century.

A Software Application Checklist

1. Adobe Photoshop
Photoshop is the best photo-image-editing software available; no other application really matches it. Vector-based illustrators need to drop in and out of Photoshop at some point and it offers a variety of formats to save files into, all compatible with other applications.

2. Adobe Illustrator or Macromedia Freehand
Every illustrator creating digital images will need to use the services of a vector application. Drawing lines and shapes and filling objects with colour with scalable perfection are the attributes that these two applications offer.

3. Macromedia Flash
For those illustrators who aim to create images for the Web this is the software that brings Freehand's static skills to life with movement. Increasing numbers of websites are built in Flash or in Dreamweaver with Flash components.

4. Adobe Streamline
When using a digital camera to capture reference material or for getting people to pose for figure work, this application helps trace around photographs and convert the result into vector line images ready for importing into a vector application.

5. A Browser
Whichever Internet facility you choose, from Netscape to Safari, make it work hard for you. Start to bookmark websites that provide useful information or reference material. Don't forget the image search facility in Google for very fast reference gathering.

6. A Mail Application
Keeping an email address book up to date is crucial. Emailing regular clients low-res attachments of recent work is a useful way of keeping in touch and providing low-cost self-promotion.

7. Adobe Acrobat
Use Acrobat to create PDFs of artwork ready for print. Locked layers ensure that it is impossible for clients to meddle with your artwork after delivery. Art directors and designers are increasingly happy to accept this format of artwork.

8. Microsoft Office
Create templates for letters, invoices, and address labels etc. This is the software that everyone in business uses, so use it to open emailed project briefs, 99% of which are sent as Word attachments. Create presentations for clients in Powerpoint.

9. A Database Application
Set up a database of clients so that you can post samples, cards, invites etc. or just keep an up-to-date record of addresses and phone numbers. Arrange fields in your database to gather as much information as you will ever need and set up to print directly on to address labels too.

10. A Book-Keeping Application
You have a duty to the taxman as soon as you start earning money from illustration. Set the records straight right from the start: it is always advisable to be creative in your image-making and not your tax returns!

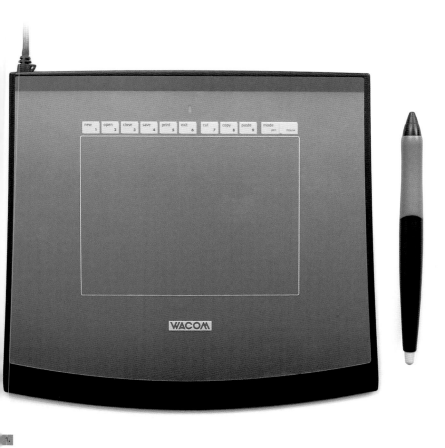

1.

Digital Essentials

1. A drawing tablet and stylo replaces mouse and mouse mat for more accurate drawing control

2. An external hard drive is vital for digital storage and back-up

3. The mouse is the fastest way of moving on-screen, although not to be used for accurate detailed work

4. CD/DVDs provide long-term digital storage of artwork and reference material

5. A digital camera is vital for shooting and recording reference materials and visuals, as well as in-putting photographic images into artwork

6. A mini keyring USB storage device is handy if your work files are not that large.

Mac/PC? The arguments remain, but work with the platform that you feel offers a more intuitive working environment – the same ruling can be applied to software too. Seek recommendations from colleagues and friends, and read reviews in the computing press to keep up to date with developments in software and hardware. Expect to upgrade to new kit every 18–24 months.

2.

3.

4.

5.

6.

Studio Set-Up

Solo or Group?

There is an important decision that every illustrator must make; it can be dictated by working methods, by financial considerations or by personal choice and it is about the location of the studio. For some the studio will be, at its simplest, the kitchen table or the back bedroom, while for others it may be a rented desk space within a design company, or a shared loft-style studio in a cool part of town. Finding the place that best suits your needs is fundamental to creating an environment conducive to creative working. Setting up a studio can be challenging and exciting, but planning ahead is crucial.

Freelance illustration is a predominately solo discipline; much of the work is undertaken in a space away from the client and delivered at the end of the process. Until email became the normal mode of delivery, illustrators tended to migrate towards the cities where most commissions were likely to be forthcoming. If they chose not to and lived and worked in another part of the country, they adjusted their working methods to allow for delivery times. Although email has made delivery an instant option and the mobile phone has ensured that communication can be a constant, many illustrators still prefer to work in urban areas. This may be related to the need or desire to meet face-to-face with the art director or designer on a project, or it may go back to issues of self-promotion and the ease in getting to and from presentations laden with a portfolio.

Deciding on a solo or group studio is determined by choice. Many illustrators demand the solace and silence of a space that is uninterrupted by fellow artists, whilst others find it impossible to concentrate without the buzz and noise of a shared space. It is wise not to rush into the excitement of creating a group studio without having had some experience of working in one. Equally, spending time and money converting a spare bedroom into a studio, if completely unused to working alone, can be a commitment and undertaking that proves to be unnecessary.

There are benefits and drawbacks to both types of studio set-up and both need some careful consideration. Working alongside others can provide an environment that is inspiring, interesting and supportive. It can also be off-putting and disturbing as well as frustrating. For those that choose to work alone, the benefits of the solo studio may be in the freedom and personal space that the situation allows. Drawbacks, however, include having no face-to-face, one-to-one conversations or feedback about an idea or work-in-progress from a sympathetic ear. Hours may pass without direct communication with another individual, although for many this situation may be a positive asset.

For those who choose to join or set up a group studio, having costs of shared equipment and facilities can be financially beneficial and can lead to greater access to technology that may be out of reach for the solo trader. Buying one very good digital camera, renting a photocopier, installing a mini-kitchen or investing in a table tennis table are far simpler spread across a group.

Communication Tools

Whether going it alone or joining a group there are some essentials that require immediate attention. Having a mobile phone, with credit, is a must, as is a studio phone that can divert to the mobile. Increasingly mobiles have email technology built into them and this can be a real plus when out at appointments for an entire day; some clients' first choice for communication is email.

A fast Internet link is not to be overlooked, sending artwork via email attachment, especially large files, can take valuable time. Occasionally company firewalls bounce emails back, if they don't recognise the sender or the file sizes are too large. Managing these issues without a wide bandwidth can take crucial time when delivering work.

➡

Shared Work Space – Pros

• Support and advice available from fellow studio members is on hand constantly.

• Shared costs of rent, equipment, phone lines as well as courier services.

• Moving from the relatively social surroundings of the art school studio to a shared studio is less of a culture shock.

• Joint marketing and promotional opportunities, as well as exhibitions and publications can be organised easily and are more financially viable when responsibilities and costs are shared across a group.

Shared Work Space – Cons

• Ensuring that a studio has a conducive working atmosphere can be tricky.

• Taking on the commitment of a shared studio is a big responsibility, especially when starting out and flow of work is not guaranteed. Signing a six- or 12-month lease can become a financial stranglehold.

• A shared space can mean compromising on the set-up in order for all members to be content in the arrangement – your desk may be next to the toilet or too near to the kitchen.

• A larger space can mean a greater risk of burglary and security issues can be a headache to resolve, as well as being potentially expensive.

• Your collection of Eastern European tin toys and Japanese Manga figures surrounding your desk may seem like an ideal setting for you, but considered a childish whimsy by others.

The Shared Work Space

1 Storage
Good strong storage is a must. It can be built-in or constructed from flat-pack, so choose based on how long you intend to be in the space.

2 Chair
Ensure that the chair that you use is comfortable and supportive – back and neck problems will follow otherwise.

3 Screen
Whether CRT or flat-screen, ensure that it is at the correct height and that it is colour-corrected. Take regular breaks – eye strain should be guarded against to prevent long-term damage.

4 Desk
Ensure that this is the correct height, and that it is level and large enough for everything that you regularly use to be within easy reach. A curved cut-away style can aid movement.

5 Cutting mat
If you are using a scalpel or knife to cut or trim paper, card or collage elements, or even to trim tear-sheets before placing into a portfolio, you need a cutting mat and a clean, even and level surface on which to place it.

The Work Space

Work spaces vary but an illustrator's studio is rarely a dull place. Digital technology appeared to turn creative design studios into sterile office environments with huge casings of grey and cream plastic, housing humming computer kit and monitors. The illustrator's studio, in contrast, appears to have retained much of the fun and frivolity of the art school. It is a fact that design groups have to entertain their clients, who may be deeply concerned to enter a less-than-professional environment, whereas illustrators create spaces they feel comfortable working in. Without the pressure of visiting clients, the studio becomes an extension of creative expression for the illustrator. It is not uncommon to see wild collections of stuffed animals, toys and model kits, thrift-store ceramics, comic art posters, rubber stamp kits and the like adorning the walls and shelves of the studio.

Illustrators can be messy; paints, inks, scraps of tracing paper, masking tape, glues, coloured crayons and sticky-backed paper are likely to be strewn across many surfaces. It is in amongst this variety of old-school materials that the computer and related peripherals sit.

Safety Issues

Setting up a work space that performs properly, that allows for creativity, experimentation and the everyday work tasks of creating illustrations needs to be done with a number of factors in mind. A dedicated space for thinking, researching and the tasks of invoicing and payment chasing, as well as portfolio organisation, must be part of the equation. Taking into account health and safety considerations such as correct height of monitor and keyboard position to ensure unharmful posture, are as important as ensuring safe working practices are adopted for the handling of potential hazardous materials such as spray paints and adhesives. Positioning a monitor away from direct light and making sure that electrical cables are not trailing across a floor are all requirements of a working space.

The Solo Work Space

1 Storage
Even within small, converted bedroom studios, storage is essential. Put up shelves to lift items away from working surfaces. Put frequently used items in easy-to-reach places and those less vital on higher shelves. It pays to plan your studio before embarking on its construction.

2 Working surface
Allow enough deskspace for monitor, keyboard, drawing tablet and scanner. The computer itself and the printer can be positioned out of the way – you are less likely to need to access these constantly.

3 Printer
A very good quality printer can be extremely expensive. Although a standard A4 digital printer is a relatively cheap initial purchase and adequate for portfolio work, these are less than ideal for use in analogue artwork. Watch out for the escalating cost of ink cartridges.

It is not uncommon to see wild collections of stuffed animals, toys and model kits, thrift-store ceramics, comic art posters, rubber stamp kits and the like adorning the walls and shelves of the studio.

Resources and Reference

Illustrators need inspiration and reference material. The notion that artists pick ideas and themes out of thin air and then create visuals without referring to real or photographed imagery is one held by some clients, but the reality is somewhat different.

Every illustrator builds his or her own reference library, whether trawling second hand bookstores for out-of-print examples of 1970s' car manuals, or out shooting and collecting photographic reference of street signage, an illustrator constantly adds to the library of images and ephemera. Old DIY magazines, instructional leaflets, stamp collections, record sleeves, matchbox labels; they are all collected and referenced.

Housing collections and libraries is never easy, as illustrators tend to require organised space to store and display objects and files as a particular colour combination or layout may be called upon at any time for inspiration. Some illustrators use storage boxes, some create large archive files for printed ephemera to be contained in, but whichever type of device or system utilised, it plays a vital part in the process of creating illustrations.

With hard drives increasing in capacity on an annual basis, storing digital photographic reference is becoming easier and many are turning to this method of organising their research. Many illustrators, however, would argue that there is no real substitute for the real object, feeling the quality of the paper, breathing in the scent of that print and handling a real object are part of the process of inspiration.

Referencing a particular image has never been quicker or simpler – huge royalty-free files of photographic reference and imagery are available on collections of CDs, the same is true for clip art and Victorian engravings and most are available from book stores, computer warehouses, traditional art and design suppliers as well as the Internet, of course. Searching for visual reference on-line takes seconds with the Google image search, one of the most important research tools to emerge for the illustrator in the last decade.

1. Scrapbooks

Pasting or sticking 'found' ephemera into ready-bound books is a useful way of keeping a collection of potential reference pieces in a manageable and coherent order.

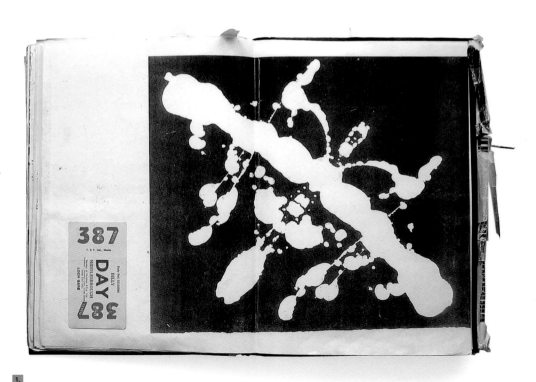

1.

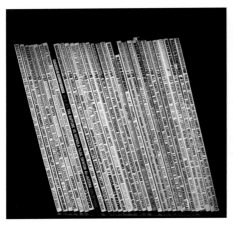

1.

2.

3.

4.

5.

6.

7.

8.

9.

eference

Magazines are great research tools

nd photographs of figures to be utilised
s visual reference for poses to draw
om or just for seeking inspiration.

Clip art and royalty-free image
ollections

lways a useful place to turn to for
particular image or icon.

Music

/orking to music can be a creative
esource – many illustrators claim to
reate their best work whilst listening to
spirational music.

Graphic design and illustration
howcases

/hilst it is never a good idea to 'borrow'
reative influences, it is wise to keep
breast of conceptual and stylistic
evelopments.

Themed reference books

ncreasingly available, these books are
acked with full-colour photographic
isual reference material themed around
articular subjects. Need to get a sense
f India in a flash for example? – this is
our solution.

Industry magazines

Jp-to-date information about current
rends and developments and also the
lace to find potential clients.

7. Art and design history books

Having a knowledge and understanding
f art and design history is vital to
comprehending how visual
communication works.

8. Software manuals

Everyone gets stuck with software issues
at some point, even hardened
professionals. Get out of a fix quickly
with the help of the right expert advice.

9. Oversized and 3D reference

A quaint piece of packaging, a novel and
collectable cereal pack give-away toy
– both potentially useful reference
material that when stored in a padded
envelope will not get broken or dusty.

10.

Reference

10. A4 display books/folders

Some visual reference may have to be
scanned, so placing it in display books
or in plastic sleeves gives protection and
easy access.

Filing, archiving and storing reference
resources in formats that are easy to
access and up to date is a fundamental
aspect of a positive studio culture. Start
as you mean to go on – make sure that
items are clearly labelled and are
ordered coherently, as this will pay off
as your collection grows. Time wasted
searching for a particular piece of
reference that eludes discovery could
have been better used chasing payment
from accounts departments, or
brainstorming a new project, or
marketing to new clients, the list goes
on.

Thrift Shop Finds

1. Second-hand bookshop finds on motorbikes and cars

Scouring flea markets, car-boot sales, jumble sales and second-hand bookshops will always throw up a range of fascinating titles from a bygone era. Depending on this method of researching whilst in the research and development period of an ongoing project can be risky however – there are no guarantees of discovering the right material. Frequent excursions to find materials of interest can be a better starting point – the books that you find are always likely to come in use at a later date.

There is no substitute for the real object – feeling the quality of the paper, breathing in the scent of that print and handling a real object are part of the process of inspiration.

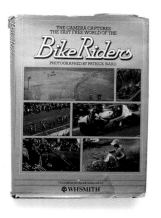

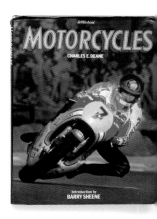

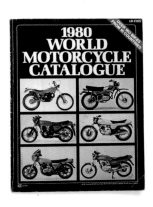

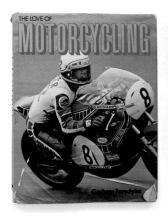

1.

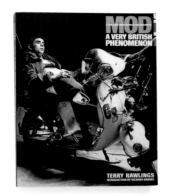

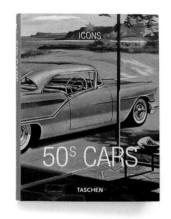

Production Tips

There are enough potential production tips to warrant filling an entire book, and shelves groan under the weight of titles offering readers purported shortcuts to learning and then mastering software. There are also numerous magazines that go on monthly sale offering software tricks and tips to readers, but many of the most frequent lessons and some of the best advice are often not highlighted or tailored specifically for illustrators. There is very little substitute for learning on the job and valuable experience gained throughout initial projects can be put to greater use as commissions appear more regularly.

Working in the field of illustration requires some specialist knowledge and for the beginner it can feel like a minefield. The best advice is to learn some technical terms and the terminology used in print and production, and understand what they all mean. If you are not sure what 'bleed' (when an image is printed to the edge of the paper) is, for example, don't be afraid to ask. It is common to meet designers and art directors that use production terms and phrases so regularly that they can forget that newcomers may not yet fully grasp the language. Never leave a briefing, however, without a full understanding of the technical expectations; mistakes can be time-consuming and costly so ensure that communication is clear or fully explained and if not, ask.

Colour Management

Start as you mean to go on and ensure that files are set up correctly before you commence a project, it is far better to do this before getting in too deep. A common mistake is to ignore the file formats required for the production of the artwork at the design stage. Set up files for print in CMYK, this breaks colours into percentages that can be achieved from the four-colour set of cyan (C), magenta (M), yellow (Y) and black (K) and is how most colour jobs are printed.

Special Colours

On some occasions fifth and sixth colours are added to the print process and these are known as 'Specials' and have to be specified correctly from Pantone reference charts. Special colours are used when it is impossible to create a colour from the four-colour set, such as metallics or fluorescents, or when it is vital to match an existing colour that needs to appear in its purest form. Specified special colours are mixed by hand and applied on a separate plate from the four plates made for CMYK. Specials are only likely to be used for specialist projects; it is not possible to specify silver ink for an illustration to accompany a magazine article, for example. It may be appropriate, though, to discuss the possibility for an image of a magazine cover, but this discussion should take place with the art director at the briefing stage and not just presented as a secondary thought with the final artwork. Adding special colours always adds to the print and production costs.

Screen-Based Work

To prepare work that will not be printed, but will always exist solely on-screen, websites, TV, animation: set files up in the RGB format. All colours are then created from properties and combinations of the red (R), green (G) and blue (B). Red, green and blue are the primary colours of light and are referred to as primary colours or as the additive primaries. Although the RGB format works for screen-based illustration projects, it is wise not to trust the representation of colours on your monitor unless it has been well calibrated. Once calibrated, a good monitor will reproduce colours for screen accurately but will always present an approximation of any project that will be going to print. It is therefore important to check the percentage breakdown of each colour used against a Pantone print swatch guide or against printed examples from previous projects.

File Formats

File formats are important to get right; ensure that you only give the client flattened images without access to the individual layers that make up the project. This gives the illustrator some protection against misuse by a client and it is best not to provide temptation. Ensuring changes or alterations required are made by the illustrator alone is the goal and files that allow clients freedom to scale and print, but not open and alter are the safest option. The illustrator retains copyright on every image they create, unless otherwise stated, and not allowing others to alter or change an image offers some protection against illustrations appearing in print that devalue the work of the illustrator.

The final file format is dependent on the type of project – some clients prefer artwork to arrive as a TIFF (Tagged Image File Format), others request JPEGs (Joint Photographic Experts Group), or EPS (Encapsulated PostScript) files; the only true course of action is to check before embarking on the project. Ensure that the resolution is correct too; creating a piece of work in 72 dpi when it is expected in 300 dpi is a common, but easily avoidable mistake. Most production issues can be resolved through tight communication; a lapse and the results can be unexpected, unwanted and unbelievable.

Setting up a Document Correctly

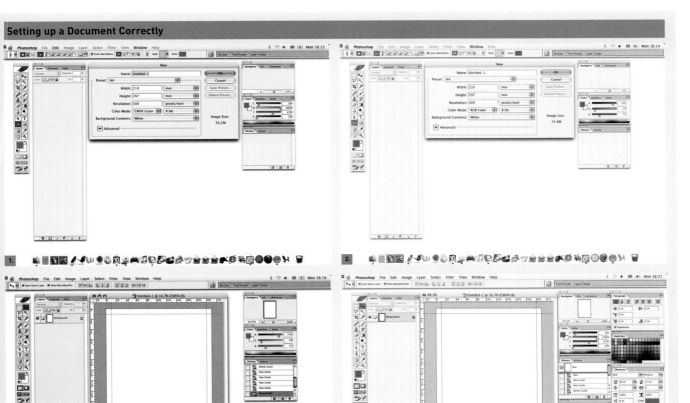

1. Start as you mean to go on

Note how, when opening a new Photoshop file for instance, the Color Mode allows for a range of options – choose carefully. Set up your document correctly by working in as high a resolution as possible, and take into account how your work is going to be used. Preparing work that will be printed using the four-colour process means creating a file in CMYK.

2. Choosing RGB

Choose RGB when your work will be used solely on-screen. This includes work for websites, TV, animation and all other digital viewing methods. Remember that the fluorescent effects of RGB colours will never reproduce accurately when the standard four-colour print process is used, so if your work is for both screen and print environments, default to CMYK, or check how the CMYK version of your RGB work will look when printed.

3. Working area

Always create your illustration to a specified size – a good brief will identify this. Use your application's rulers to give a perfect indication of how the final piece will look. Set up any 'bleed'; when an image is to run right to the edge of the page, the file should give 0.5mm of extra image at each edge to allow for trimming inaccuracies. Here this is laid out using rulers (in red).

4. Palettes

When creating an illustration in any application it is a very good idea to arrange your working area so that it suits the way in which you best perform. Lay out the palettes that you will most use, clear away those that are superfluous to demand and if you have access to a second monitor, consider placing all extras on to the second desktop. Not so much a luxury, but increasingly a necessity.

The CMYK Colour Printing Process

1. Yellow Printer
2. Magenta Printer
3. Cyan Printer
4. Black Printer
5. Yellow Proof
6. Magenta Proof
7. Cyan Proof
8. Black Proof
9. Yellow Proof
10. Yellow + Magenta
11. Yellow + Magenta + Cyan
12. Yellow + Magenta + Cyan + Black

The colour printing process uses four main colours – cyan, magenta, yellow and black. These colours are printed in sequence as a tiny series of dots, that in combination reproduce the full colour range of the original image. The image must be colour separated before the process can take place – the examples show the various combinations that can be reached using the four-colour set.

Additive Primaries

Colour reproduction is based on the three-colour vision of the human eye. Three receptors in the eye recognise the primary colours of light – red, green and blue. White light is made up of all three primary colours, as when added together they create white – these are the additive primaries. When only two of the additive primaries are combined, they create one of the subtractive primaries as shown in this illustration.

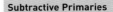

Subtractive Primaries

The subtractive primaries – cyan, magenta and yellow – are created by removing one of the additive primaries. When all three subtractive primaries are combined, they produce black. The subtractive primaries are the same three process colours used in printing – a full-colour image is made by creating 'separations' – translating an original into CMY and Black, added because of limitations of ink pigments.

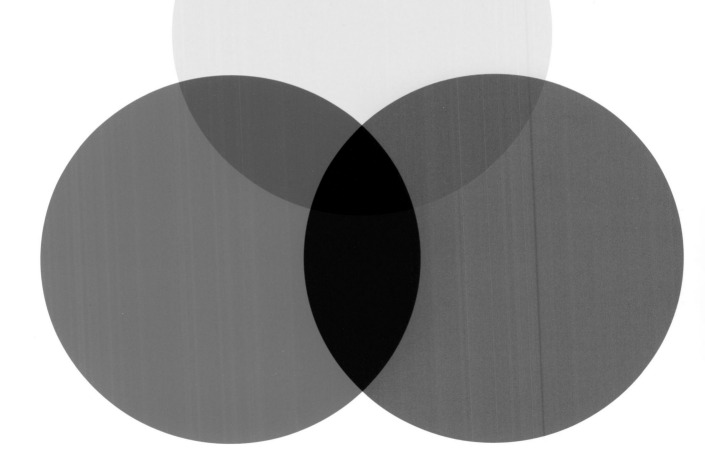

Saving A Document Correctly

1.

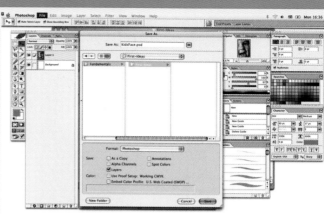

2.

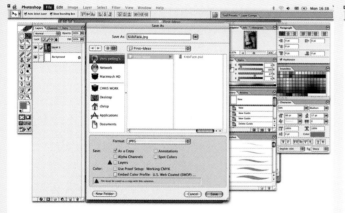

3.

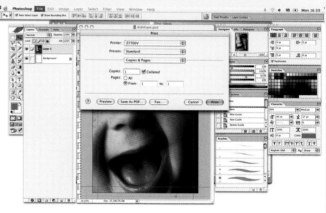

4.

1. Safe saving

It is far safer to get into the habit of saving your work on a regular basis right from the start of a project. When opening a new document, save it immediately. Create a new project folder that can include all elements – the brief, any notes, digital photographic reference and scanned elements, as well as the artwork file.

2. Safer saving

As well as saving your work into a folder on your hard drive, you'll need to get into the regular habit of backing up your work. Burning work on a regular basis to CD or DVD can be time consuming, but is an essential aspect of digital storage. Some illustrators ensure that they store digital files in two places – at home, as well as their studio so as to reduce the risk of loss through fire.

3. File formats

Saving your work can appear to be a complex issue with the range of options available within most software applications. A good rule of thumb is to save as a JPEG, an EPS or as a TIFF. Each has its benefits and drawbacks, but for vector images, go for an EPS, for photographic use JPEG, or TIFF if your image has lots of halftones.

4. PDFs

A file format option that many illustrators have adopted as more and more repro houses begin to accept it is the PDF – Adobe's Portable Document Reader as the software needed to open a PDF and it is available free of charge. Acrobat Reader has enabled users to open any file that has first been saved as a PDF – most applications now offering it as a 'Save As' feature.

Legalities

An often overlooked aspect of the day-to-day running and long-term organisation of a career in illustration is in the legalities and liabilities surrounding tax issues. Despite illustration rarely falling into a list of careers that have difficulties in keeping the right side of the law, it is wise to know and fully understand all potential implications associated with the legalities.

If you plan to work in illustration, then it is vital to ensure that your local tax office knows that you are trading for business. There is an unwritten rule that states that creative people have problems with numbers, figures and maths – get yourself organised early and ensure that you set your business up correctly from the start.

Firstly find your local tax office and turn to them for advice about exactly how you should set up your business – make sure that all events are taken into account. Normally you'll not be expected to pay any tax until your annual turnover reaches a certain level – this can be hit quite soon if you get busy, so be prepared.

Enlist the services of an accountant – take advice and recommendations from other illustrators. Use someone who has some understanding of the profession and the possible implications for your tax issues. A good accountant will recommend particular courses of action, explaining pitfalls before they arise and pointing out methods of eliminating unnecessary tax burdens. They may command a hefty fee for their services, but that expense should be paid for out of the savings they make you.

➡

Your Name Here
Your Postal Address
Should Go Into This Space
Postcode
Your Telephone Number
Your Contact Email
Your Website Address

invoice

number:	0101
date:	31–12–05
client:	Company Name of Client Client's Address Should go Here Including Post/Zip Code in Full
contact:	Your point of contact within the company: the person and their title that commissioned you
order number:	Some companies will give you an Order Number that you must quote on your invoice
job number:	Some companies will also give you a Job Number too
description:	Describe in full what the commission was
fee:	State agreed fee here
expenses:	State agreed expenses here
TOTAL DUE:	State final amount owing
terms:	State payment terms and to whom cheque should be paid to
copyright:	State copyright ownership

1.

ACCEPTANCE OF COMMISSION

To..................
I am pleased to accept your commission for artwork as follows:

Title/Subject:
Commissioned By:
Delivery Dates:
Roughs:
Artwork:
Fee: £/$
Plus VAT:
Expenses: £/$

TERMS OF COPYRIGHT LICENCE TO BE GRANTED

Customer:
Use:
Area covered by Licence:
Duration:
Exclusive/Non-Exclusive:
Credits
A credit for non-editorial work is required if this box is checked
(see Clause 23 overleaf)
Special Terms (if any):

The Standard Terms and Conditions for this commission and for the later licencing of any rights are shown on the back of this page. Please review them together with the above and let me know immediately if you have any objection or queries. Otherwise it will be understood that you have accepted them.

THIS COMMISSION IS SUBJECT TO ALL TERMS AND CONDITIONS ON THE REVERSE SIDE

Signature of Illustrator:
Date:

Invoicing (I)

1. Sample invoice

A job doesn't end with the delivery of the artwork – billing for work and then following up with reminder phone calls, sadly a regular occurrence, is another aspect to the job of illustrator. Create an invoice that is easy to read and has all the vital information visible – name, address and contact details, as well as commission information and fee with any agreed extras.

2. Acceptance of commission form

Good practice in the relationship between the commissioner (the art director) and the commissioned (the illustrator) should involve, as standard procedure, an agreement in writing to protect both parties. A wise initiative on the part of the illustrator is to send an Acceptance of Commission Form stating information about the project – delivery dates for visuals and then for artwork, agreed fees, details regarding ownership of copyright etc.

2.

An accountant will advise you of exactly what details your invoice should cover – obvious details include your name and address. Less obvious details, but as important is that the invoice carries an invoice number – a legal requirement. An accountant can also advise you of terms and conditions that you may wish to apply to your clients, although further expertise can also be sought from a solicitor.

Access to a good solicitor will come in handy should you need information and advice regarding copyright issues – ensuring that you retain copyright over your images is a fundamental right. Working out exactly what to charge for usage or for full copyright of an image can be tricky – an agent can come in handy here or at least advice from a solicitor with links to a professional industry body such as the Association of Illustrators or the Society of Illustrators.

Ignorance is no defence – make sure that you fully understand just how to set your business up legally. Being aware of what to do and not do is vital – be prepared.

TERMS & CONDITIONS

Ownership of Copyright/Copyright Licence

1. The copyright in artwork commissioned by the Client shall be retained by the Illustrator.
2. The Client or the Client's customer (where the Client is acting as an intermediary) is granted a licence to reproduce the artwork solely for the purposes set out on the face of this acceptance of commission. If the acceptance of commission is silent, the Client or the Client's customer is granted an exclusive licence for one time use in the United Kingdom only.
3. During the currency of the licence the Illustrator shall notify the Client of any proposed exploitation of the artwork for purposes other than self-promotion and the Client shall have the right to make reasonable objections if such exploitation is likely to be detrimental to the business of the Client or the Client's customer.
4. Where use of the artwork is restricted, the Illustrator will nominally grant the Client or the Client's customer a licence for use for other purposes subject to payment of a further fee in line with current licensing rates to be mutually agreed between the Illustrator and Client.
5. The licence hereby granted to use the artwork is contingent upon the Illustrator having received payment in full of all monies due to her/him and no reproduction or publication rights are granted unless and until all sums due under this Agreement have been paid.
6. The licence hereby granted is personal to the Client or the Client's customer (where the Client is acting as an intermediary) and the rights may not be assigned or sub-licensed to third parties without the Illustrator's consent.

Payment

7. The Client shall pay all invoices within 30 days of their receipt. Interest at a rate of 2% per month is payable on any balance unpaid after 30 days of the date of invoice.

Cancellation

8. If a commission is cancelled by the Client, the Client shall pay a cancellation fee as follows:
(i) 25% of the agreed fee if the commission is cancelled before delivery of roughs;
(ii) 33% of the agreed fee if the commission is cancelled at the rough stage:
(iii) 100% of the agreed fee if the commission is cancelled on the delivery of artwork;
(iv) pro rata if the commission is cancelled at an intermediate stage.
9. In the event of cancellation, ownership of all rights granted under this Agreement shall revert to the Illustrator unless the artwork is based on the Client's visual or otherwise agreed.

Delivery

10. The Illustrator shall use her/his best endeavours to deliver the artwork to the Client by the agreed date and shall notify the Client of any anticipated delay at the first opportunity in which case the Client may (unless the delay is the fault of the Client) make time of the essence and cancel the commission without payment in the event of the Illustrator failing to meet the agreed date.
11. THE ILLUSTRATOR SHALL NOT BE LIABLE FOR ANY CONSEQUENTIAL LOSS OR DAMAGES ARISING FROM LATE DELIVERY OF THE ARTWORK.
12. The Client shall make an immediate objection upon delivery if the artwork is not in accordance with the brief. If such objection is not received by the Illustrator within 21 days of delivery of artwork it shall be conclusively presumed that the artwork is acceptable.

Approval/Rejection

13. Should the artwork fail to satisfy, the Client may reject the artwork upon payment of a rejection fee as follows:
(i) 25% of the agreed fee if the artwork is rejected at the rough stage.
(ii) 50% of the agreed fee if the artwork is rejected on delivery.
14. In the event of rejection, ownership of all rights granted under this Agreement shall revert to the Illustrator unless the artwork is based on the Client's visual or otherwise agreed.

1.

Changes

15. If the Client changes the brief and requires subsequent changes, additions or variations, the Illustrator may require additional consideration for such work. The Illustrator may refuse to carry out changes, additions or variations which substantially change the nature of the commission.

Warranties

16. Except where artwork is based on reference material or visuals supplied by the Client or where otherwise agreed, the Illustrator warrants that the artwork is original and does not infringe any existing copyright and further warrants that she/he has not used the artwork elsewhere.
17. The Client warrants that any necessary permissions have been obtained for the agreed use of reference material or visuals supplied by the Client or its customer and shall indemnify the Illustrator against any and all claims and expenses including reasonable legal fees arising from the Illustrator's use of any materials provided by the Client or its customer.

Ownership of Artwork

18. The Illustrator shall retain ownership of all artwork (including roughs and other materials) delivered to the Client.19. The Illustrator's original artwork shall not be intentionally destroyed, damaged, altered, retouched, modified or changed in any way whatsoever without the written consent of the Illustrator.
20. The Client shall return all artwork to the Illustrator not later than 6 months after delivery in undamaged, unaltered and unretouched condition although the Client may make and retain transparencies to enable it to exploit the rights granted with the artwork.
21. If the artwork is lost or damaged at any time whilst in the Client's custody (which shall mean anytime between delivery of artwork to the Client and its safe return to the Illustrator) the Client shall pay compensation to the Illustrator for the loss/damage of the artwork at a rate to be agreed or, in default of agreement.
22. THE CLIENT SHALL NOT BE LIABLE FOR ANY CONSEQUENTIAL LOSS OR DAMAGES ARISING FROM LOSS OR DAMAGE TO THE ARTWORK.

Credits/Moral Rights

23. The Client shall ensure the Illustrator is credited in any editorial use of the artwork. Credits for non-editorial use are not required unless so indicated on the front of the form.
24. The Illustrator hereby waives the right to injunctive relief for breaches of the right of integrity and the right of paternity.

Samples

25. Unless otherwise agreed, the Illustrator shall be entitled to receive not less than four proofs or printed copies of the work.

Notices

26. All notices shall be sent to the Illustrator and to the Client at the address stated in this Agreement. Each party shall give written notification of any change of address to the other party prior to the date of such change.

Governing Law

27. These terms and conditions are governed by the law of England and Wales, or your country of residence and may not be varied except by agreement in writing. The parties hereto submit to the non-exclusive jurisdiction of the English Courts.

Copyright

1. Terms and conditions

On the reverse of the standard Acceptance of Commission Form can be printed a set of terms and conditions defining the fuller details of issues such as copyright licence and ownership, approval and rejection of artwork, changes to artwork and even ownership of the artwork itself pertinent to the laws of your country of residence. If your client agrees to these terms, it can be safe to assume that they can be trusted to act professionally.

Contacts

Will Ainley
will@willainley.co.uk
www.willainley.co.uk

Kenneth Andersson
info@kennethandersson.com
www.kennethandersson.com
www.eyecandy.co.uk

Jody Barton
work@jodybarton.co.uk
www.jodybarton.co.uk

Luke Best
luke@lukebest.com
www.lukebest.com
www.peepshow.org.uk

Mr Bingo
bingo@mr-bingo.co.uk
www.mr-bingo.co.uk

Andrew Brandou
meowdy@pacbell.net
www.howdypardner.com

Jon Burgerman
jon@jonburgerman.com
www.jonburgerman.com
www.biro-web.com
www.blackconvoy.com

Paul Burgess
punkrock.paul@virgin.net
www.paulburgessart.co.uk

Anthony Burrill
anthony@friendchip.com
www.anthonyburrill.com

Brian Cairns
Brian Cairns Studio
brian@briancairns.com
www.briancairns.com
www.friendandjohnson.com

Paul Davis
Big Orange
davis@copyrightdavis.com
www.copyrightdavis.com
www.mapltd.com
www.agentform.se

Miles Donovan
m@milesdonovan.co.uk
www.milesdonovan.co.uk
www.peepshow.org.uk
www.blackconvoy.com
www.art-dept.com

Fafi
fafi@fafi.net
www.fafi.net

Sara Fanelli
sara@sarafanelli.com
www.sarafanelli.com

Jason Ford
j.ford@macunlimited.net

Pete Fowler
fowler.p@virgin.net
www.monsterism.net

Nicholas di Genova
Triclops Studio
medium@mediumphobic.com
www.mediumphobic.com

Michael Gillette
m.gillette@sbcglobal.net
www.michaelgillette.com

Jasper Goodall
jasper.goodall@sukie.co.uk
www.jaspergoodall.com
www.bigactive.com
www.jg4b.com

Jenni Grey
jennigret@btinternet.com

Justin Hampton
665@justinhampton.com
www.justinhampton.com

Han Hoogerbrugge
han@hoogerbrugge.com
www.hoogerbrugge.com

Margaret Huber
m.huber@mac.com

Insect
Paul Insect
info@insect.co.uk
www.insect.co.uk

JAke
DETONATOR studio
jakesteel@btinternet.com
www.jake-art.com

Billie-Jean
sam@billiejean.co.uk
www.billiejean.co.uk

Jeremyville
jeremy@jeremyville.com
www.jeremyville.com

Adrian Johnson
info@adrianjohnson.org.uk
www.adrianjohnson.org.uk
www.centralillustration.com
www.blackconvoy.com

Joel Lardner
joellardner.com
heartagency.com

Chrissie Macdonald
chrissie@chrissiemacdonald.co.uk
www.chrissiemacdonald.co.uk
www.peepshow.org.uk

Satoshi Matsuzawa
mail@salboma.com
www.salboma.com

Richard May
rich@richard-may.com
www.richard-may.com
www.art-dept.com

McFaul
john@mcfaul.biz
www.mcfaul.biz
www.centralillustration.com
www.ba-reps.com
www.blackconvoy.com

Roderick Mills
roderick@roderickmills.com
www.heartagency.com

Neal Murren
neal_murren@yahoo.co.uk
www.nealmurren.com

NEW
theStudio@NEW-online.co.uk
www.new-online.co.uk

Izumi Nogawa
G-DIA@quietblue.org
www.quietblue.org

Henry Obasi
henry@ppaint.net
www.henryobasi.com
www.ppaint.net

Kristian Olson
K.O.A.D.
kristian@kristianolson.com
www.kristianolson.com
www.centralillustration.com

Matt Pattinson
Culprit Art
mattpatt.520@virgin.net
www.culprit-art.com
www.stickernation.net
www.crushed.co.uk

Simon Pemberton
simon@simonpemberton.com
www.simonpemberton.com

Pinky
pinky@misterpinks.com
www.misterpinks.com

Gary Powell
garybpowell@hotmail.com

Stina Persson
stina@stinapersson.com
www.stinapersson.com

Andrew Rae
a@andrewrae.org.uk
www.andrewrae.org.uk
www.peepshow.org.uk
www.blackconvoy.com

Graham Rawle
questions@grahamrawle.com
www.grahamrawle.com

Jay Ryan
the bird machine, inc.
posters@thebirdmachine.com
www.thebirdmachine.com

Kustaa Saksi
kustaa@kustaasaksi.com
www.kustaasaksi.com
www.unit.nl
www.louisebertaux.com

Rosie Scott
rosiescott@fastmail.co.uk
www.rosiescott.co.uk

Matt Sewell
mattsewell@jacuzzi.fsnet.co.uk
www.mattsewell.co.uk

Andy Smith
asmithillustration
andy@asmithillustration.com
www.asmithillustration.com

Ray Smith
www.raysmith.bz
www.happinessatwork.org
www.centralillustration.com

Michiko Tachimoto
info@colobockle.jp
www.colobockle.jp

Tado
Mike Doney and Katie Tang
mikeandkatie@tado.co.uk
www.tado.co.uk

James Taylor
printzoo@dircon.co.uk
www.printzoo.co.uk
www.debutart.com

Elliot Thoburn
ethoburn@btinternet.com
www.peepshow.org.uk
www.off-centre.com/art.asp

Will Tomlinson
info@williamtomlinson.com
www.williamtomlinson.com

Vault 49
Jonathan Kenyon & John Glasgow
info@vault49.com
www.vault49.com
www.roulefashion.com

Akira Wakui
akira@wakuiweb.com
www.wakuiweb.com

Chris Watson
chris@strega.demon.co.uk
www.chris-watson.co.uk
www.TonUpPress.com

Louise Weir
Studio 32
louise@louiseweir.com
www.louiseweir.com

Autumn Whitehurst
awhitehurst@acedsl.com
www.altpick.com
www.art-dept.com

Spencer Wilson
spencer@spencerwilson.co.uk
www.spencerwilson.co.uk
www.synergyart.co.uk
www.peepshow.org.uk

Ian Wright
mail@mrianwright.co.uk
www.mrianwright.co.uk

Bibliography

Selected Books

The Beatles Illustrated Lyrics
Alan Aldridge
Little, Brown

The Big Book of Illustration Ideas
Roger Walton
Harper Design International

Clin D-Oeil – A New Look at Modern
Illustration
Adam Pointer
Book Industry Services (BIS)

The Complete Guide to Digital
Illustration
Steve Caplin and Adam Banks
Ilex

Contact Illustrators and Visionists
Nicholas Gould
Elfande

Digital Illustration – A Masterclass in
Creative Image-Making
Lawrence Zeegen
RotoVision

The Education of the Illustrator
Steven Heller and Marshall Arisman
Allworth Press and the School of
Visual Arts

Fashion Illustration Now
Laird Borrelli
Thames & Hudson

Fashion Illustration Next
Laird Borrelli
Thames & Hudson

The Fundamentals of Creative
Design
Gavin Ambrose and Paul Harris
AVA Publishing SA

Hand to Eye – Contemporary
Illustration
Angus Hyland and Roanne Bell
Laurence King Publishing

Head Heart & Hips – The Seductive
World of Big Active
Gerald Saint
Die Gestalten Verlag

Imagemakers – Cutting Edge
Fashion Illustration
Martin Dawber
Mitchell Beazley

Pen and Mouse – Commercial Art
and Digital Illustration
Angus Hyland
Laurence King Publishing

Pictoplasma
Peter Thaler
Die Gestalten Verlag

Pictoplasma 2
Peter Thaler
Die Gestalten Verlag

Picture Perfect – Fusions of
Illustration and Design
Ian Noble
RotoVision

Rewind – Forty Years of Design and
Advertising
Jeremy Myerson and Graham
Vickers
Phaidon Press Limited

Selected Websites

Organisations:

The Association of Illustrators
www.theaoi.com

The Society of Illustrators
www.societyillustrators.org

Agencies:

Advocate Art
www.advocate-art.com

Central Illustration Agency
www.centralillustration.com

ZeegenRush
www.zeegenrush.com